Scottish Abbeys

Scottish Abbeys

An Introduction to the mediæval Abbeys
and Priories of Scotland

STEWART CRUDEN, ARIBA, FSA
Inspector of Ancient Monuments for Scotland

EDINBURGH
HER MAJESTY'S STATIONERY OFFICE
1960

First published 1960

Third Impression 1970

Printed in Scotland for Her Majesty's Stationery Office
by R. & R. Clark Ltd., Edinburgh. Dd. 239047/1333 K.48

SBN 11 490475 8

Contents

List of Illustrations

The illustration on the wrapper shows a detail of the sculpured angel lintel over the great west doorway of Holyrood

" 'Did you ever see an old abbey before,
    Mr Peters ?' 'Yes, miss, a French one; we have
    one at Ramsgate; he teaches the Miss Joneses
    to parley-voo, and is turned of sixty'."
    THE INGOLDSBY LEGENDS (1906), p. 8.

Introduction

To most people a ruined abbey is an enigma. The remains arouse interest but do not satisfy curiosity, even when completeness is restored in the mind's eye, and that is difficult enough with buildings so extensive and complex 'all knocked downe to desolation'. Puzzled by the size and complexity of the buildings and the strangeness of the life they represent, the visitor is likely to leave the site somewhat at a loss and with a suspicion that they are capable of a rational if not a simple explanation.

It is easier to picture an imagined life in a mediaeval castle than in a monastery which existed at the same time as the castle, and which might indeed have been built by the same men. In the little sunny court of a small castle Henry James lay upon the grass and enjoyed 'the sensation of dropping back personally into the past'. And we all do, and picnic the more easily amidst drum towers and battlements than we do beside a nave arcade. Though there is no doubt about the imagined picture of life in a mediaeval castle, even when details in the contemporary scene are lacking, much doubt attends the visitor to a monastery. One wishes to know why there were so many buildings in it, how many monks it contained, what manner of men they were and what they did all the time in their small world. Did they do any good, or are they to be dismissed as selfish escapists? Questions such as these, about people, rarely occur during visits to ancient castles. Similarities to ourselves are there generously assumed and differences as easily dismissed. With a little historical sense and some imaginative effort we identify ourselves in the contemporary scene, but a ruined

monastery presents questions which too often defy explanation and leave the visitor unsatisfied.

This is natural enough. The monastic life is inevitably
strange to the layman. Yet those who have enjoyed the pleasure of visiting monasteries of our own day are instantly im-
pressed, and doubtless surprised, by the cheerful ordinariness
of the monks. This indeed is the root of the matter. Monasteries are nothing if not practical. Designed by 'master-
masons' whom we would today call architects, skilled and
experienced men who had learnt their art at the benches and
in the lodges of masons and carpenters, these great edifices
served severely practical ends. So successfully did they do it
that an architect recently engaged in restoring a thirteenth-
century monastery for re-use by Cistercian monks told the
present writer that try as he would to depart from the
mediaeval plan in deference to contemporary taste, he was
continually drawn back to it as the most workable solution to
his own problems. He touched upon an enduring fact there:
with little change or concession to modern requirements
the monastery of today is much the same as it was in the
Middle Ages. It exists to house a community of monks whose
way of life is unchanging, to furnish accommodation for
them, and to provide for needs and duties which remain
much as they were eight hundred years ago.

Mediaeval abbeys of different periods and different
monastic orders were basically very much alike. A monk
from one could without difficulty find his way about another.
The church, the cloisters, the dining hall, dormitory,
offices, storage cellars and so on were by and large similarly
arranged. In appearance, in the design and details of the
buildings, they naturally differed somewhat. Sculptural
enrichment, arrangement of windows and their mouldings,
arcades, roof coverings, the degree of austerity or elaboration
of the whole, all these varied according to custom, skill,
whim, locality, date or architectural fashion. But wind and
weather, warfare, neglect and stone-robbing have reduced
our monasteries to ruins in such wayward fashion that each

now appears to have been entirely different from the others. This is misleading. It is the purpose of this book to assist understanding and increase appreciation of our ruined abbeys by offering an explanation, in general terms and as simple as can be, of monasticism and monastic buildings.[1]

A word about definition might not be out of place here. 'Monastery' and 'convent' are equal terms of general reference. In more particular use 'convent' means the inhabitants, the corporate body of monks, as opposed to the buildings. It does not carry the feminine meaning of today; a religious house of women was a 'nunnery'. Monasteries might be abbeys, priories or dependent houses (or cells) in that order of importance. It is a question of status. An abbey is a monastery whose head was a monk with the rank of abbot (*abbas*, father) and the next in seniority was the monk who had been elected prior. A priory was ruled by a prior. In purpose and function, in number of monks and size of buildings there need be no visible difference, although generally an abbey tends to be the larger establishment, suitable to the higher status of its superior, but this is not necessarily so. In the great monastic order of Cluny, for example, only the original house (the mother-house, or parent-house) of that name was an abbey, all the offshoots or daughter-houses were priories, even though many exceeded abbeys of other orders in size, wealth and importance. This subordination of the Cluniac houses, wherever they might be and however powerful they might be, is an expression of and a result of the strongly centralised administrative organisation which was characteristic of that order.

Some observations about ruins and ancient buildings

[1] Hence the lack of plans, without which no book about architecture is worthy of its subject. There are only two. That of Melrose shows the complexity of a large monastery, that of Dundrennan gives a typical lay-out and illustrates the general description in the text (pp. 41-48). Official Guide-books with detailed plans are available for most monuments.

might likewise assist the visitor. The very fact that so much is reduced to foundations can be turned to advantage, for it permits an appreciation of lay-out which would be the more difficult if not impossible to achieve were the buildings complete. An imaginative effort should be made to reconstruct in the mind's eye an impression of enclosure, to visualise buildings rising bulkily about one; to see open spaces as small courtyards and alleys between them; to imagine interiors, enclosed and roofed. The details do not greatly matter, the important thing is to see the monastery in solid bulk, not in ruins of draughty arches. Even the church was closely partitioned by massive stone walls and timber screens separating aisles, choir, nave and altars.

To assist imagination and illustrate this important matter of enclosure conjectural restoration drawings of selected abbeys have been made with the greatest possible accuracy in the light of the evidence afforded by surviving masonry.[1] The lay-out as shown on these drawings is reliable, for it is based on surviving foundations which tell their tale even if only a foot high. The upper parts and details are trustworthy where evidence exists. In other parts they are conjectural, but feasible. For parts where no evidence exists, (*eg* a spire) the features are simplified.

As no Scottish monastic site is anything like complete what remains upstanding at one site should be recollected at another. Every piece of evidence is of value. No impression should be left behind as though it belonged to its own site alone. It should be stored in the mind's eye for recollection elsewhere. It must also be remembered that most ancient buildings are of many periods, and that their life in any one period has probably been eventful. An abbey ruin today might well represent two or three hundred years of building activity. Even the simplest building is not so simple as it seems to be.

With a working knowledge of the basic elements of a

[1] These are available as post-cards for Melrose, Dundrennan, Jedburgh and Dryburgh. (Pls. 13, 16, 22 and 30).

monastic lay-out, and with the increasing experience of visits the observant visitor will soon be able to identify instantly the various parts which survive, will note and identify the evidence of missing parts, however fragmentary it might be, and with particular satisfaction will welcome parts hitherto unencountered.

In the description of Scottish abbeys which follows, attention will be drawn to the notable parts of each monument, and to what each particularly has to offer, but before proceeding to the more detailed although brief account of these still imposing and evocative ruins and the life they represent some general observations might usefully be made to clear away some misconceptions which obstruct a proper understanding of monasteries.

By and large they housed comparatively few monks. Early zeal attracted the requisite numbers to the parent-house and ensured success for what must always have been an adventurous undertaking. Later periods of prosperity also created unusual popularity. But for various reasons numbers declined. Monks were drawn from the parent-house to colonise daughter-houses, and they in their turn, when established and having attracted more brethren, themselves became parent-houses. On the whole, monasteries contained considerably fewer monks than the size and distinction of their buildings might lead one to suppose.

Now architecture and sculpture are powerful auxiliaries of belief and mediaeval man was a true believer, even when he only feared and trembled. The church touched his life at every point, in every day. However wayward he might be its spiritual authority was unchallenged. All nature was of God's creation, the monster as much as the angel. This is the simple explanation of the frequently puzzling occurrence of the incongruous sculptured figures which sound such telling notes and animate the architecture (Pls. 14 and 15). The mediaeval sculptor recognised no modern distinctions of propriety. Explanations which advance theories of artisan mischief and irreverence to account for the apparent incongruity and unseemliness of grotesque beasts, comical, commonplace, vulgar and even blasphemous figures in the vicinity of the high altar, the sculptured saints and the Virgin Mary, regard the disturbing objects through twentieth-century eyes and with the modern prejudices which separate the lay from the ecclesiastical.

Humour and bright colour are conspicuous in all mediaeval art. The margins of the elaborately illustrated books, Bibles and other religious works are alive with fanciful creatures, dragons and grotesques, every-day scenes and monkeys playing tricks. The hinged seats of choir stalls afforded the wood-carver free expression for his fancy, and he drew upon the world around him for his subject matter. Scenes of sport, domestic life, the romantic tales of strolling players, mythical and spurious beasts all inspired his skill in carving the under side of the tip-up seats which allowed the comfort of sitting with the appearance of standing in the long choir services. Outside, in the shelter of the church porch, the 'miracle' and 'morality' plays presented the same mixture, and conveyed the Christian message with moving simplicity and directness not entirely innocent of knock-about humour.

Evidently there was no impropriety in mingling laughter with religion, nor in revealing the deep obsessions of a scarcely-forgotten pagan past, until St Bernard of Clairvaux despatched the great Cistercian mission, and *c* 1134, denounced visual beauty and condemned these obscene monkeys, these battling warriors, these horn-blowing hunters, this deformed beauty, this beautiful deformity. And yet he granted some concession to the ignorant, some easy appeal to the senses, and moreover made of his polemic a literary work of art.

Repentance could snatch a sinful soul from the gaping jaws of hell, that monstrous Leviathan consuming the damned which was so frequently sculptured over the great doorways of churches for the edification of the beholder;

and prayer and supplication could shorten the years of purgatory and hasten the everlasting beatitude; not only one's own prayers, but those of monks and priests for oneself and one's descendants and friends, and prayers could be ensured by benefactions. It has been said that 'from one point of view the whole vast organisation of the mediaeval Christian church can be regarded as the result of man's fear of eternal damnation and his desire for eternal bliss'.

The view which denies the monk his full measure of esteem on the grounds that his life is unproductive is surely thoughtless and superficial, for although mediaeval monasteries, according to the rule of St Benedict from which they were all derived, existed for the service of God and the spiritual welfare of their inmates, and for no other reason, their very existence in a troubled world whose only enduring institution was the church was of the greatest possible benefit not only to the welfare of the State but to individuals in every walk of mediaeval life. Up to the middle of the thirteenth-century the monastic life was considered to be the ideal form of the Christian life. Mediaeval chroniclers used the word 'religion' in the restricted technical sense of monasticism, a 'religious' as one who had taken the monastic vows and, 'conversion' as meaning to enter a monastic order.[1] Whatever motives of spiritual self-interest induced men and women to take monastic vows or to achieve credit vicariously by endowments and benefactions, the end in view was pious, and however much the monasteries fell away in the performance of their high purpose, that purpose was the worship of God.

The decline of the monastic ideal need not be discussed in this volume and will not be except as it affected monastic architecture. That architecture can be studied like any other, in terms of structure, form following function, and so on. But it is comprehensively and significantly a religious architecture, expressing in some monasteries the austere

---

[1] Conversely, a non-monastic cleric was a 'secular', a non-monastic church was a 'secular' church.

ideals of the early Cistercians in a white-walled simplicity, in others the decorative fancies which they had rejected, and in all the ritual of the divine office and the discipline of the cloister. We may conclude with words of another modern writer, useful to remember 'If men's hearts, a thousand years ago, were practically the same as ours, yet their actions were often strangely different; because nature or society put very different obstacles in their way, and promised them success by paths which often differed widely from ours'.

The Origins of Monasticism

The Middle Ages, particularly the twelfth century, was the great period of monasticism in western Europe. The largest Scottish abbeys were founded in this century, and none after Sweetheart in 1273, but there were others before them.

From earliest times there have been men and women who believed that only by withdrawing from the world and its worldliness and by living a dedicated life of devotion and self-denial could they save their souls. In this renunciation lies the essential spirit of monasticism, which was early apparent in the deserts of Egypt and Syria where, for long, holy men had lived alone, practising great austerities. Alexandria was then a centre of Christian thought. It was also a great and rich city with harmful temptations to alarm the devout. Great numbers of what one might call Christian spiritual refugees flocked to the wilderness to emulate pagan ascetics there before them. The first of the desert fathers known to us by name were St Paul and St Anthony whose meeting in the desert c250 AD is commemorated on more than one of our Pictish sculptured stones.

As their number increased from the middle of the third century they built their cells within reach of each other and thus formed groups, especially in the Egyptian deserts where c320 St Pachomius established the first Christian community. By 350 AD there were thousands of Christian hermits in the deserts who sought perfection in solitude, penance and prayer.

For the individual recluse in the wilderness no formal behaviour or organised way of life was necessary, but his was a soul which was ill at ease, sustained and exhausted by

fervour. Groups of kindred spirits could the more easily
fulfil their spiritual tasks by submitting themselves to a common discipline, which would ensure not only the opportunity for prayer and contemplation, but also an atmosphere
of ordered peace and tranquillity in which it could be
attained.

The different conceptions of individual salvation and
communal living were reconciled in a written constitution
which was to have enduring influence throughout the
Middle Ages and even to our own times. This was the code,
or Rule, of St Benedict, and it was written *c* 529. It modified
the eremetical ideal of the East with its excessive emphasis on
physical ascetism and provided a system more suited to
western temperaments and requirements. It is not long, but
it deals with every aspect of monastic life and government
with such profound wisdom that all monastic orders of the
Middle Ages followed its principles of absolute regularity,
strict discipline and unvarying routine, albeit with some
differences of emphasis and interpretation. The church of the
Celtic civilisation of the far West did not. Cut off from
the Continent by the barbarian invasions which followed
the evacuation of England by the legions in the early fifth
century, it continued a rule-less existence until its decline in
the late seventh century.

Monastic life of the type prevalent in Italy, and at least a
knowledge of the rule of Benedict were introduced into
England by St Augustine in 597, but the formal introduction
and application of the Rule is attributed to Wilfred, a monk
of Lindisfarne, upon his return from Rome in 658. With
Wilfred there had travelled to Rome another Northumbrian
monk, Benedict Biscop, a Northumbrian nobleman who had
forsaken his patrician life to enter the Benedictine monastery
at Lérins, near Cannes, which had become one of the great
centres of the Christian church in France in the fifth century.
Biscop returned to Canterbury in 669 to become abbot of
the monastery of St Peter and St Paul. The south-east of
England thus received another strong impact of Benedictine

monasticism some seventy years after Augustine's landing. From the late sixth century, therefore, Christianity and an organised monasticism which was governed by a rule and sustained by all the power of direct papal encouragement made headway in England notwithstanding inevitable set-backs. Eventually it came into conflict with the monastic church of the Celtic West.

The Celtic Monasteries

In the long period when Britain was a province of the Roman Empire it was in close touch with the Continent where Christian monasteries in the eastern tradition were numerous. When and from where the first missionaries came to Britain is uncertain. The names and dates of but a few are known. They include St Alban, who suffered martyrdom in 304, shortly before Christianity was recognised by the emperor Constantine. Thereafter it enjoyed toleration if not general acceptance. Certainly there was an organised church in England, with bishops, before the Roman occupation ceased in the early years of the fifth century. At this time the first datable Celtic monastery in Britain was founded by St Ninian, probably *c*400, at Whithorn in Wigtownshire.[1] Ninian dedicated his little church to St Martin, founder of the renowned Gaulish monastery at Tours where he had doubtless received instruction. Towards the middle of the fifth century St Patrick, son of a Roman provincial official, and also the product of a Gaulish monastery, Marmoutier, extended the ascetic and eremetical monasticism of Gaul to Ireland. In 563 St Columba left Ireland to found his famous Irish Celtic monastery on Iona. From Iona the Celtic church entered Northumbria at the invitation of a Northumbrian king who had once sought refuge there.

[1] The origins of Christianity in Scotland are so obscure as to be even beyond conjecture in the present state of our knowledge, and the history of St Ninian and Whithorn is highly controversial. The statements made here are necessarily brief but not necessarily accurate. They follow the conventional dating which has long depended on a twelfth-century *Vita* of Ninian by Ailred of Rievaulx, and the eighth-century *History* by Bede.

The historic landing of Augustine in Kent in 597 there-fore comes late in the history of the early church in Britain, but it came as the first purposeful and sustained missionary enterprise from Rome, at the instigation of the pope himself, and it came to the eventual discomfiture of the Celtic church which had achieved so much before it.

Northumbria was the meeting place of the expanding Roman and Celtic churches. They were at variance in or-ganisation and observance, for the severance of the Celtic church from the Continent during the prolonged barbarian invasions of the Dark Ages caused it to develop—or not to develop—in isolation. It was out of step with the church of Rome, and by the end of the sixth century it was wholly monastic, which the Roman church was not and its monasti-cism was loosely organised, alien to the Benedictine rule and perpetuated much of oriental tradition. Admirably suited as centres of learning, for which they became famed throughout Christendom, and as training centres for fearless and saintly men whose lonely holiness and distant wanderings to win converts for Christ appeal so strongly to the imagination, the Celtic monasteries were bound to give way to the more regular, stable and disciplined ways of life introduced and practised by the monks of St Benedict. The Celtic monastic church established no permanent non-monastic churches to administer to the converted. The Christian rites were performed in the course of long and arduous journeys by monks and priests who eventually returned to their mon-asteries. Such a system was well suited to missionary en-deavour but not at all to provide for the permanent religious needs of a newly converted community whose faith required support and encouragement. The Celtic church declined. It withdrew to the West from which it had emerged, and by the end of the seventh century its days were numbered.

Yet its influence endured, particularly in art and tradi-tions of learning. Works of great beauty and splendour, intricate and intensely Celtic, were created in stone, metal and manuscript. The richness, sophistication and superb

technical skill of the Celtic artistic achievement is in striking
contrast with the architecture of the monasteries which
produced it in such amazing abundance, and with the
conditions of inconceivable discomfort in which it was
created in our long northern winters. When, in the eighth
century, Abbot Cuthbert of Wearmouth was late in sending
copies of Bede's works to the archbishop of Mainz, he
explained that the hands of the scribes were so numbed by
the bitter winter weather that they had been obliged to
interrupt their work for considerable periods. 'Cold has
caught the wings of birds, season of ice—these are my
tidings' wrote a scribe; and another, to relieve the tedium of
copying, poetically penned an idle thought in the margin of
his manuscript thus 'Pleasant is the glint of the sun today
upon these margins because it flickers so'.

Although a reference to Celtic monasticism is only of
marginal interest in such a brief account as this must be
the story of abbeys in Scotland would not be complete
without it, for it was peculiar to the Celtic West and
abundantly represented in Scotland a form of monasticism,
which even if routed by the Benedictines, had a long and
heroic history going back to the earliest days of monasticism
in Bible lands; and it was invested with more of the original
fervour and spirit than was the mediaeval form of monasticism with which we are most concerned.

Perhaps an instinctive sympathy with the defeated
attracts our first affections. Perhaps also the lack of buildings
to engage our attention emphasises the personal aspect of
Celtic monasticism which is such a conspicuous feature of it,
and which is exemplified in these most human and poetic
quotations from the immense heritage of early Christian
literature which the so-called Dark Ages has bequeathed
to us.

From their poems and the stories of their lives, their nar-
ratives of travel, hardship and penitential exile we perceive
the influence of the individual. As we read Bede's *History of
the English Church and People* (c730), we understand King

Edwin sitting alone for hours wondering which religion he should follow; we visualise the tense scene as the heathen high priest rides out before him and his thanes to defy their God—and then destroys his own altars; and we stand beside King Oswald as he sets up a great oaken cross with his own hands and summons his army to prayer before battle with the heathen. And in another narrative we sense the drama of the conflict in the story of the old pagan chieftain who died of rage upon hearing of the passion of Christ.

The earliest Celtic monasteries were analagous to the *lauras* of the desert fathers and consisted of a few hermits' cells grouped about a small oratory. A saintly hermit might receive land or a fort from a converted or tolerant chieftain. The ramparts of the pagan fort provided protection and an appropriate symbol of separation from the outside world. Bede relates how St Cuthbert came from Melrose to the Farne Islands and ordered evil spirits to withdraw, so that his island became quite habitable 'And when he had expelled these hostile forces, the brethren helped him to build a tiny dwelling surrounded with a ditch, and such essential buildings as an oratory and a communal shelter'.

But little by little crowds of pilgrims and disciples invaded these hidden retreats, so that in the early ninth century it was written 'The little places where hermits settled two together, three together, are now resorts of pilgrims where hundreds, where thousands assemble'. Such communities were in the West the nearest approach to the town or city, and with the art and learning of the Irish and Scottish monasteries carried to Iceland, the Faröes, Shetland and all over the Continent they were primitive universities too, books had almost magical virtues, and writing in itself was held in superstitious reverence. The text of scriptural works especially was quite overwhelmed by the elaborate art of giant initial letters and portraits of the evangelists, the literary expression of the spirit which arrayed shrines and reliquaries in gold and precious stones. 'I send my little dripping pen unceasingly over an assemblage of books of great beauty to enrich the possessions of men of art—whence my hand is weary with writing'.

The foundation of a mediaeval church on the site of an earlier Celtic church, and even its erection on the actual ruins of the earlier church, is quite consistent with the religious spirit of the early Middle Ages. The site was holy, the new church absorbed its sanctity. The mediaeval cathedrals of Winchester, Canterbury, Durham, Glasgow and Whithorn, for example, are all closely associated with early saints and their relics, which in the mediaeval revival were translated to imposing shrines in the new churches. And if the saints' relics received especial veneration, so did the tomb of the mediaeval founder of an abbey, as it had done in Celtic times, when a great cross or cross-slab was erected near the primitive church to mark his grave and tomb.

Place-names such as Kilmichael, Kilmartin, Kilmory, Kilchattan, suggest a Celtic settlement of some sort; a chapel (*Kil-*), or oratory, or preaching station, with a dwelling nearby, and a connection, not necessarily first-hand, with the commemorated saint.[1] They indicate the spread of the Celtic church and the spheres of influence of its most distinguished servants. They do not prove the presence of the saint himself nor even of the disciples who worked in his name, but they afford strong presumptive evidence of their endeavours in the district, it being customary for the followers of a saint of outstanding renown to name their own foundations after their master, as Ninian did when he named Whithorn after Martin of Tours. Sites and localities have yielded material relics which corroborate the evidence of such place-names. For example, Kilmichael Glassary, Argyll, has yielded a Celtic bell, now on view in the National Museum of Antiquities in Edinburgh; in the churchyard of

---

[1] The Celtic saint is not to be confused with the canonised saint of the mediaeval Roman church. There were three orders or degrees of Celtic sainthood. Almost without exception Celtic saints were hermits or monks. As the Irish monasteries were clannish or tribal the Celtic status of sainthood came perilously near to being hereditary.

Kilmartin nearby there are two early sculptured crosses: in the ruined mediaeval priory at Ardchattan[1] there is still a splendid early Christian cross-slab: assuredly there was a Celtic settlement there which the Valliscaulian monks were pleased to revive. The concurrence of archaeological and historical evidence in association with place-names is sufficiently frequent to be convincing: such Celtic place-names indicate Celtic sites of some sort, whether or not there is anything to be seen of them today.

Whithorn, Wigtownshire

Of the sites which survive and which have been excavated unquestionably the most important is St Ninian's at Whithorn, which is in the care of the Ministry of Public Building and Works. History, archaeology and building are each unusually well-represented here. The founding of Ninian's monastery in the locality is not disputed, although its date is.[2] A number of Celtic crosses are preserved in the site museum, including the oldest Christian monument in Scotland, of *c* 450. Recent excavations have revealed half of Ninian's church. It emerges from beneath the east gable of the mediaeval church which succeeded it. Thus Whithorn demonstrates extremely well the mediaeval custom of erecting new churches upon hallowed sites, and the translation of relics from one to another, for it is known that the shrine of St Ninian was moved into the new church there to remain a renowned place of pilgrimage until the Reformation.

The walls of the early church stand about three feet high and still retain the white plaster which anticipated the mediaeval practice of limewashing and plastering walls all over, about which a Cluniac monk wrote *c* 1003 'It was as if the whole earth, having cast off the old by shaking itself, were clothing itself everywhere in the white robe of the church'. The notion of rendering ancient walls with plaster is generally unwelcome to modern ideas which have been influenced by experience of stony ruination. But such was

[1] See below, p. 90.   [2] See above, p. 12, footnote.

the treatment. St Wilfred in the seventh century gloried in having washed the York Minster of his day 'whiter than snow', a Saxon abbot of Peterborough boasted that he had so skilfully white-washed his cathedral that it appeared as if cut out of one single stone, and a Welsh mediaeval chronicler saw churches scattered over the land so that it shone like a firmament with stars.

Bede took note of the unusual style of Ninian's church 'commonly known as *Candida Casa* the White House, [Whitherne, Whithorn] because he built the church of stone, which was unusual among the Britons'. As dry-stone churches were not uncommon in the north country where native stone was easily available and required no great skill to use it was surely the white plaster which attracted Bede's notice. The discovery and identification of this primitive little church of the early fifth century, in the middle of a Celtic monastery and beneath the sanctuary of the twelfth century cathedral-priory is one of the most notable contributions of the archaeologist to the history of the Christian church in Britain. This simple little plastered building must indeed be the church which St Ninian made about two hundred years before St Augustine landed in Kent, and over one hundred years before St Columba landed on Iona, and it is here that his body and those of many saints lay at rest for so many centuries.

Nothing has been identified of the enclosing cashel wall by which the limits of the Celtic monastery can be determined. It was doubtless extensive. Stones dating from the mid-fifth to the seventh century have been found in the locality and are in the priory museum and at Kirkmadrine nearby there are more in the care of the Ministry, in the porch of the disused parish church which was erected on the site in modern times, doubtless upon or near to an ancient foundation. In the museum are several from a cave at Physgill, three miles away, whose walls bear a further series of votive crosses, cut in the rock. Evidently this was a retreat, a *disert*, to which, according to contemporary accounts of

St Martin's monastery at Tours, the monks withdrew for periods of lonely contemplation and even greater hardships than their monastery provided.

Iona, Argyll

A cashel wall is a distinguishing and prominent feature in several other Celtic sites. At Iona, a site of peculiar interest in the history of the early church, not only in Scotland but in all Christian Europe, the *vallum monasterii* is clearly definable for some considerable distance round its circuit.

Iona was an Irish monastery, founded by St Columba in 563. He was not the first churchman on the island, but its fame dates from his rule. Scholars were attracted to it from near and far, by the renown of the saint himself and by the growing influence of the monastery as a school and missionary centre of European reputation. It was not the only large and populous monastery in the Celtic world. The fame of Clonmacnoise, Clonfert, Glendalough, Bangor, and other Irish monasteries was great and likewise attracted foreign saints and scholars, but Iona claims a special place in our history because of Columba and all we know of his life. A splendid series of Celtic crosses and sculptured stones, and a legend testifying to many more, survive as witness to his monastery, but of the monastic buildings, many of which were of wood, only doubtful evidence has been recovered in recent excavations, and it is unlikely that the oratories and cells, the barns and refectories, will ever be found. The *vallum monasterii* is therefore of much importance.

Birsay, Orkney

In the far north, at the north point of the Orkney mainland, an off-shore island known as the Brough of Birsay has been excavated by the Ministry. It is a remarkable site of early Christian, Viking and mediaeval remains. A cemetery of Celtic monks has been uncovered. It yielded a Pictish symbol stone of unusual interest at the head of a triple grave.

Three bearded and distinguished laymen are featured. They are well appointed and bear shields and spears. On the same surface are three Pictish symbols and what could be a totem eagle. Three graves, three warriors, three symbols; this is the most significant association of a Pictish symbol stone with graves which has so far been found and it supports the theory that these enigmatic symbols describe the status or office of the dead they are presumed to commemorate. It also assists dating.

With the Ninianic endeavour continuing from *c*400 and the Columban from 563 there is a likelihood of the evangelised parts of Scotland being Christian by *c*600. Although the symbols are not religious but secular, and may have a pagan ancestry, they are used in a Christian context. Now even the Church at its most tolerant would not permit their erection fifty or seventy-five years (two or three generations) after conversion. Lapses from orthodoxy would be, and were, allowed to first converts, but the Church's eyes and aspirations were on the children, who, indoctrinated by Christian teaching, would in fifty years or so be in power. Lapses by them when adult would be treated with clerical severity, be it even the king himself who lapsed. The stone could hardly have been erected after *c*650-75, which dates the beginning of this remarkable northern settlement. Of the early Christian church only partial foundations running beneath an eleventh-century Christian Norse church can be discerned, but considerable traces of the surrounding cashel wall have been uncovered.

Arran, Bute
On the island of Arran another site in the Ministry's charge, at Kilpatrick, comprises a large area within a high earthen bank which encloses the foundations of buildings.

Eileach-an-Naoimh, Argyll
On this small and uninhabited rocky island, one of the remote and unpopulated group known as the Garvellachs,

in the Firth of Lorne, is a remarkable early Christian site which has survived in greater height and extent than any other. It is also in the care of the Ministry. It consists of walled enclosures, two churches, a barn, a granary and other buildings, and, perhaps most interesting survival of all, a double-chambered beehive cell. Not all of the remains are of one date, and it is not yet possible to attribute any part to the time of St Brendan, in whose *Vita* the site is referred to as *insula Aileach*. An extract from a paper on the site by Dr W. Douglas Simpson is worth quoting in full. He says:

> It was while in retreat upon this island, in or about the year 573 AD, that Columba found it borne in upon him, with such an intensity of conviction that he felt himself yielding to an angelic command, that it was his duty to ordain Aedhan MacGabhran King of Dalriada. It was Aedhan MacGabhran who restored the struggling fortunes of the little Scotic kingdom, and paved its way to ultimate supremacy over the Picts of Alba. And it is from Aedhan, King of Dalriada, that her present Majesty Queen Elizabeth, traces her descent, through Kenneth Macalpin, the House of Canmore, and the Stewarts. Not only this, but the consecration of Columba's nominee, which duly followed at Iona, is the oldest record of a royal consecration known in Western Europe. If such great events flowed from a vision vouchsafed to St Columba upon our remote island in the Garvellochs, then surely this group of early Celtic monastic ruins, even supposing that no one of them can be dated back to Columba's time, is invested with a sanctity and an interest perhaps without parallel in Scotland, saving only Iona and Whithorn.

There is little doubt that this is the Hinba of Adamnan and later chroniclers, and as little of pre-Columban monasticism has come down to us (Whithorn is the notable exception) the potential importance of the site is much increased.

St Ninian's Isle, Shetland

In the south of Shetland a small site bearing the suggestive name of St Ninian's Isle was recently explored. Although it is improbable that Ninian himself was here, the existence of the name in such a part was sufficient to cause investigation. A small church was uncovered, surrounded by an earthen bank, and by happy chance a most remarkable hoard of silver of eighth-century date was found buried within the church.

St Blane's Church and Monastery, Bute

In 558 the Irish monastery of Bangor was founded by St Comgall. It became a renowned centre of Christianity. St Blane of Kingarth, in Bute, was trained there at the hands of St Comgall himself. He returned to Kingarth to rejoin his uncle St Cathan from whom the district of Kilchattan takes its name. Blane succeeded his uncle as abbot of a monastery and died *c*590. The monastery flourished, and its list of abbots extends to the year 790, at which time the Viking devastations began. Thereafter it passes from the written record. St Blane's church today is a ruined twelfth-century unaisled edifice within a small cemetery containing mediaeval grave-stones. Near it is a circular 'ring-fort' and sundry grass-grown foundations of the Celtic monastic buildings. All are contained by a lengthy cashel or enclosure wall.

The cemetery is in two parts, an upper and a lower. The lower cemetery was for long known as the women's cemetery and as late as 1661 the presbytery of Dunoon, after a customary visitation to the parish, delivered a stern rebuke and enforcement against the superstitious custom of burying men and women separately in two different churchyards. The practice (in which there surely resides a recollection of Celtic or even pagan custom) was however persistent, and the minister was instructed to make the act effectual by carefully attending burials for a season to resist the continuance of transgression. In the lower cemetery is a small oblong building orientated east and west, which could be a Celtic oratory.

The massive circular stone wall of the 'ring-fort', of late Iron Age or Dark Age date, is closely paralleled in two monuments in the Ministry's charge on the Island of Arran nearby. Its wall is about five feet high all round and some eight feet thick, complete in its circuit, and with the entrance preserved. It is not unlikely that this was the fort of the chieftain who, at some time in the sixth century, gave land and perhaps the fort itself to the new monastery.

The cashel wall is of stone, dry built, some three-four feet high and six feet thick. It follows an irregular course over uneven ground. It is in good condition, having been repaired by the Marquis of Bute in 1896. The gateway through the wall exists and ancient hill tracks converge upon it. A nearby rock, outside the gateway, has been roughly fashioned as a base with a socket for a great Celtic cross.

The romanesque church has an oblong nave and chancel. The chancel arch is complete and has excellent mid-twelfth century detail. The upper parts of the nave walls were somewhat restored by the marquis. They stand about eight feet high. The masonry is first-rate, and the wrought work of string courses, arch mouldings, column capitals and so on is most accomplished. It is the most substantial church in the islands of these parts and must have served not only Bute but the islands of Arran and the Cumbraes as well. It was doubtless the church of the lord of Bute and of considerable importance until the early fourteenth century, when the twelfth-century chancel was extended to its present size.

The church stands on the site of what is probably a natural eminence artificially made up to provide a more or less level surface for the cemetery. This has yielded early Christian and 'Pictish' grave-stones and headstones of tenth and eleventh-century date. The stones are most interesting historical documents for they testify to the continuing use of the cemetery from the time of its foundation in the sixth century into the Middle Ages, and furthermore, as the West was under Norse domination in the tenth and eleventh centuries, they prove the presence of converted Norsemen in Bute, into whose hands the site is likely to have fallen as a secular possession. Evidence of Christian Norse occupation of the island is of much importance, for little is known of this period of Viking and Christian history.

Outside the cemeteries, but within the enclosure wall, are grass-grown foundations of many small buildings. There is no reason to doubt that excavation will prove them to be of the Celtic monastic buildings.

The Monastic Orders

If the Celtic church created no organisation for the mediaeval church to inherit, it exemplified the original zeal and
self-denial which no succeeding monastic order ever forgot,
which few equalled, and to which all aspired to return at
one time or another in their history. 'Reform' summarises
monastic development and explains the remarkable rise and
spread of the new orders in the early twelfth century. It was
not an unknown urge. As early as the second century an
eastern sect called the Montanists left the orthodox church
because of an inconvenient puritanism and belief that the
church was already too worldly—and this when it was still
a persecuted minority. In the fifth century St Augustine of
Hippo deplored the worldliness of the church; and throughout the Dark Ages recurrent voices called for remedies to
correct error and combat abuse. By the middle of the
eighth century all parts of Britian previously adhering to the
Celtic system, which had penetrated throughout England as
well as the Celtic West, had conformed to the established,
systematic and highly organised church of Rome which
embraced the Benedictine system of monasticism. This
ensured a continuity which the expiring Celtic church could
not provide, depending as it did upon the personal enthusiasm and example of its monks, not upon the strength
inherent in an institution. Enthusiasm is an uncertain
guide, and the Benedictines knew it.

Although the Celtic church was singularly free from
charges of abuse and worldliness, and held in high esteem
by orthodox churchmen such as Bede, there is nevertheless
a suggestion of an eighth-century reform movement within

it, and it seems that the Culdees (*Célidé*) as the latter-day
Celtic monks were called, may have formed convents of
stricter and more formal discipline within the older and
laxer organisation. Less is known of the Culdees than is
known of their illustrious predecessors, and despite isolated
instances of strenuous refusal to admit defeat they were
eventually absorbed into the Augustinian order of regular canons which of all the new mediaeval orders was
the most acceptable to the native tradition.[1] Thus for the
second and last time in its history the Celtic church was
superseded by the Roman and absorbed into the Benedictine system.

The rule of St Benedict had a majestic simplicity superior
to details, but in its wisdom and adaptability was somewhat
vague and capable of different interpretations. Consequently it was difficult to translate into practice to the complete satisfaction of all Benedictines.[2] The first of the new
mediaeval houses which arose after the disruptions of the
Dark Ages was the abbey of Cluny. It early created a strict
administrative system of centralised control over dependent
or daughter-houses. It also developed, to a degree which
was never surpassed, a most elaborate and prolonged choir
service, far from simple and not at all austere. The Cluniac
day became a highly elaborate round of liturgical performance.

Apart from the difficulty of recruiting the number of
choir monks sufficient to perform the offices adequately the
emphasis on liturgy was over-much for minds drawn to
more puritanical ideals. Thus it came about that in the last
years of the eleventh century and the beginning of the
twelfth century a number of splinter groups were formed,
and these led to the foundation of 'reformed' orders.

They were not revolts from the Benedictine rule. On the
contrary, their leaders, who withdrew from their monas-

---

[1] See below, p. 37.

[2] St Benedict did not found an order. He wrote a Rule, from which
the later mediaeval orders derived their constitutions and observances.

teries to lead a solitary life of hardship and self-denial in the ancient style, all had in mind the same intention, which was not to repudiate the rule but to follow it independently along what they believed to be its true path, from which they believed the monastic life had strayed. They sought spiritual grace in greater austerity than they believed could be provided by the comprehensive Benedictine rule as it was interpreted in other religious houses. To them others of like mind were inevitably attracted, and the old pattern of solitude-community-organisation was repeated; and it was repeated yet again when the reformed orders themselves underwent an easing of austerities and a lowering of their original high standards.

For example, severe as the Carthusian discipline was it was not severe enough for Viard, a lay-brother in the monastery of Lugny in Burgundy. At the end of the twelfth century he obtained permission from his abbot to withdraw from his monastery to live the life of a recluse in a cave in the Val des Choux (*Vallis Caulium*). There he earned great renown for his austerities and devotion. Duke Odo III, about to leave for the Fourth Crusade, vowed to found a new order with Viard as abbot were he fortunate enough to survive *his* labour for the Christian faith. Thus the Valliscaulin order was founded. It was one of exceptional severity, borrowing from both Carthusian and Cistercian practice.

Apart too from individual pressure to concede some comfort and alleviate the original harshness, from monks who had no experience of the original spirit, the larger and impersonal organisation imperceptibly and inevitably changed as its contacts with the lay world outside the precinct wall increased and became more complex. A general secularisation took place, for although a gift of land was absolutely essential for the erection of the monastic buildings—the gift of a ramparted fort to a Celtic monk is an early instance of this need—endowments of land and goods more than was absolutely necessary led to a surplus and a corresponding encroachment into the religious life of the monks by the pressing demands of material affairs. Although individually the monks were dedicated to the triple vow of poverty, chastity, and obedience, the ideal of poverty was in jeopardy when the monastic body was itself a wealthy and business-like institution. Concessions to individuals came the more readily from an organisation undergoing a general secularisation.

This trend in monastic life was natural and inevitable. Indeed it was impossible to stop, for it began with bene-factions given in the spirit of true charity, the urge for expiation, and the desire for the monks' prayers. The attitude is exemplified in the twelfth century *Vita* (*Life*), of Ailred of Rievaulx, one of the outstanding Cistercians of his day. The bishop instructs him to accept grants of land from knights in generous free-alms, 'and he obeys, since he had realised that in this unsettled time such gifts profited knights and monks alike, for in those days it was hard for any to lead the good life unless they were monks or members of some religious order, so disturbed and chaotic was the land, reduced almost to a desert by the malice, slaughters and harryings of evil men.'

The danger was fully realised by Stephen Harding, the English abbot of the new Cistercian order which was foun-ded in 1098. He refused all aid. Nonetheless the Cistercians became in the course of the twelfth century one of the greatest land-owning concerns in Europe, and by *c*1210 their characteristic austerity was waning and their example no longer inspired as it had done. Only one order, the unyielding Carthusian, successfully resisted the inducements of charity throughout its long existence.

Although the original cause of twelfth-century monastic expansion was inspired by zealous and dissatisfied monks, and effected by their desire for reform and their will to bring it about, the movement was also fostered by laymen. Moved by the religious compulsion which found expression in pilgrimages and crusades a lord might wish to found a monastery. Indeed the granting of land and the founding of religious houses was a common form of private charity among the upper classes in the twelfth and thirteenth centuries, and this form of patronage had its parallel in the lay foundations of parish churches, which were held as private possessions and heritable property since Celtic and Saxon times. True piety caused this, but spiritual self-interest doubtless played its influential part, for the founder of a monastery was held in especial regard by the community he had sponsored, just as the chieftain was in early Christian times, whose gift of land, and perhaps a fort as well, had set a Celtic monastery upon its feet. And as the early founder was buried in the precinct so was the mediaeval patron buried in the choir, near the high altar, on the north side, in close proximity to some departed ecclesiastic of notable virtue. His well-being in the future life would be thus ensured. Masses for his soul and the souls of his descendants were earned by this and other benefactions. The splendid effigies and monumental brasses which dignify parish chancels today are not there because the commemorated were local dignitaries, but because they were benefactors, and had justly earned the privilege of burial in the most sacred place.

Benefactions usually took the form of a gift of land for the original buildings, and endowments of more land with its produce to maintain the community naturally followed ('one piggery with 10 sows, and 1 boar, and pasture free of charge'). Subsequent protection in time of need, and other practical demonstrations of piety were welcome and rewarded, sometimes before death, in rights to monastic hospitality and admittance to the convent where the founder or patron could spend the evening of his life in suitably religious and contemplative surroundings.

The founder might patronise some particular order through admiration of its observances, its ideals and customs. He might be impelled by gratitude for hospitality received, or in commemoration, or in fulfilment of a vow made in fear of death, or in thanksgiving for a merciful survival from shipwreck. The order favoured was not necessarily one for which the founder had any special regard, but was perhaps the nearest, or one with which he was familiar, to whose superior he would appeal for a colony of monks to settle upon his land and build their church and cloister. Such new monasteries were not always of great size, but could be small dependent houses or cells comprising but two or three monks. Initially much depended upon the generosity of the founder. The patron too played a prominent and often a decisive part in the fortunes of every monastery by representing the convent in the secular sphere, protecting its interests and promoting its welfare. He was not necessarily the same person as the 'founder', who might be a descendant of the original founder, but in practice the two were often the same.

The initiative for monastic expansion also came from established abbeys desiring to expand, to pioneer, to carry their way of Christianity further and further. Appeal would therefore be made to a lord for land, for upon his indulgence at least the success of the adventure depended. He became the founder, and in all probability the protector and continuing benefactor, or patron. A large house would begin with a colony of twelve under a superior usually with the status of prior—the sanctified number of thirteen, in recollection of Christ and his twelve apostles. Such would comprise the original establishment of a new house colonised from a parent-house already of such size that these monks could be spared.[1]

Not only the well-to-do were interested in the well-being of the local abbey, for the monastery touched the life of the surrounding countryside at many points, and we must picture our abbeys, priories and smaller houses in their rural environment of eight hundred years ago. They were utterly remote, or hard by a village, or near a town of no great size by modern standards. Around the monastic precinct wall and especially outside its gatehouse a village grew. Its

[1] *cf.* the modern history of Pluscarden, pp. 91-2.

market was held with the abbot's permission and the market cross symbolised the peace of a market held with the blessing of Holy Church. To the monastic revenues went voluntary donations from the people, from which the abbot dispensed alms and charity. (An abbot of Paisley ran a licensed tavern within the abbey precinct, to help finance a reconstruction of the church.) If the monks were withdrawn from the world to the cloister and the choir, there were nonetheless among them brethren who were necessarily in frequent touch with secular affairs and laymen, by reason of duties connected with the ordinary and everyday affairs of the convent.

The monastic life was open to all who could endure its privations.[1] From all classes of society its members were attracted, but not all could sustain the vow of stability for life. The peace of the cloister provided a refuge from the insecurity and danger of the age but the price it exacted was more than most could contemplate. To all but a few the life was unnatural. But to the professed monk, whether 'reformed' or not, it was the only life, and from the few the spiritual life of the country would recruit its leaders. We might justly add, the secular life also, as the 'religious' were almost the only literates in the early centuries: and the learning and administrative capacity which they monopolised was French. Indeed, Archbishop Lanfranc of Canterbury, an Italian, a Benedictine monk himself, one-time abbot of two great Norman monasteries, and an able administrator of William the Conqueror, regarded a monastery less as a retreat than as a university. A contributory cause of the post-conquest monastic reformation in France and Normandy was the transference of a considerable number of energetic and gifted churchmen to England in the wake of Duke William's armies, to administer English houses both new and revived. The French houses were

---

[1] 'When you wish to sleep, they wake you: when you wish to eat, they make you fast. The night is passed in praying in the church, the day in working, and there is no repose but in the refectory: and what is to be found there? Rotten eggs, beans with their pods on, and liquor fit for oxen'.

thereby weakened, deprived of their most able leaders, and the demand for reform was consequently accelerated.

Even among those who had taken vows after the lengthy novitiate which the orders wisely provided there must have been many for whom the life-long seclusion and privation were almost unendurable, and the fear of the consequences of breaking their vows more unendurable still. When, *c* 1143, a tormented monk of the Cistercian abbey of Revesby in Lincolnshire pleaded that his inconstancy was not equal to the burden of the order the abbot restrained him by irresistible moral appeal, so that the fugitive, hastening to the opened gate, felt the empty air as though it were a wall of iron.

The story of the same abbot's conversion, some ten years previously, is a very different one, and reveals the other side of the medal. By happy chance he hears how certain monks had come from across the sea and settled at Rievaulx in Yorkshire (the parent-house of Melrose). Wonderful men they were, famous adepts in the religious life, white monks by name and white in vesture (*ie* Cistercians). They venerate poverty and are as terrible as an army with banners, spurning fleshly desires of vainglory in food, drink, act, and affection. Carried away by eager desire he rushes back to his lodging, mounts his horse, and with the hastiest of farewells speeds his mount he knows not where. He is given a triumphant welcome by Walter Espec, the founder of the abbey, and meets the prior, the guestmaster and the keeper of the gate. He leaves them to accomplish his mission to the King of Scotland (David I) for he is a man of some importance, but returns, and is again met by the monks, who have a shrewd suspicion that the will of the visitor has been prompted by longing for his well-being. And so he becomes a monk, divides all his goods and abandons everything.

He became novice-master at Rievaulx, abbot of Revesby, and then abbot of Rievaulx *c* 1145; and he quenched the heat in himself of every vice by immersing his whole body in ice-cold water, which was contained in a tank hidden under the floor of the novice-house, when he was alone and undisturbed.

The Benedictines, Cluniacs and Tironensians

When Augustine and his companions landed in Kent in 597 they inaugurated a history of Benedictine monasticism which was to endure for a thousand years. The Rule was not forgotten in the dislocation of church life during the warring centuries of the Dark Ages. In the late tenth-century monastic revival it was an inheritance which revitalised the old monasteries and inspired the new. There was no Rule but the Benedictine.

One great Benedictine house, however, the Burgundian abbey of Cluny, had, in the closing years of the tenth century begun to evolve a constitutional organisation and a distinct monastic discipline, to which reference has been made in the preceding pages. The Cluniac characteristics of strict central control of dependencies and a ceaseless, solemn and elaborate ceremonial were however developed without formal severance from the Benedictine system, and these two powerful institutions, the only monastic orders in being before the reform movements of the early twelfth century, together represent the mediaeval Benedictine order.

A third member of this monastic family was created in 1109, at which time the power of Cluny was in decline. It was avowedly a reformed community which grew up about Bernard, a Benedictine monk of Poitiers, who had, in dissatisfaction with his life and monastery, taken the extreme step of resisting the abbot of Cluny. He retired to the solitude of the forest, at Tiron near Chartres. When the number of adherents who rapidly gathered about him was such that a Rule was required to regularise their life, the customs of the abbey of Cîteaux, by then about ten years old, were influential for both the Cîstercians and the Tironensians revered simplicity and desired to re-instate manual labour to its supposedly original importance in monastic life. There was a notable difference in the result. Whereas the Cistercians expressed their regard for the dignity and benefits of manual labour in field-work, the Tironensians fostered crafts and handiwork, and thus attracted artisans, who could pursue their secular avocations in the discipline of a cloistered and contemplative life. Their affiliation to the greater Benedictine order remained strong, and in Scotland they were becoming known simply as Benedictines in the later twelfth century. It is a remarkable fact that in Scotland the Tironensians were uncommonly well represented, and by major houses, whereas in England they were scarcely represented at all, by one minor house and dependencies only.

There were four large Tironensian abbeys in Scotland, and two priories; two Cluniac abbeys and one priory (including the disputed house on the Isle of May which might properly be Benedictine); and three Benedictine abbeys and three priories, and a few uncertain Benedictine dependencies.

The Cistercians

The first and one of the most eminent and influential of the 'reformed' orders was founded *c* 1098 at Cîteaux by Robert, the abbot of Molesme (an independent house which followed the customs of Cluny) and Stephen Harding, an Englishman. They withdrew from Molesme in dissatisfaction with the monastic life there, and settled in the woods of Cîteaux as hermits. Disciples gathered about them. Robert was recalled to Molesme. Stephen's genius produced the *Carta Caritatis*, the charter of spiritual love, of which a recent historian has said that it was 'perhaps the most perfect constitution for a monastic order that has ever been devised'. Stephen refused charity, rightly fearing the corrupting influence of possessions, and for about ten years the future of the new order was uncertain. In 1115 however it was joined by Bernard (not Bernard of Tiron), later to be abbot of one of the first daughter-houses, and one of the great figures of the Middle Ages. Owing to him the order spread rapidly and far. So much so that in the middle of the twelfth century there was a statutory veto against further expansion, through fear of redundancy, but this was ineffective. The new order attracted the more austerely zealous from the established Benedictine houses and hastened the decline of Cluny. The ardent reforming spirit which animated its early years inevitably brought discord to its relationships with other orders.

The Cistercians venerated poverty, not the penury of the idle and negligent but a wilful poverty sustained by faith and love. They renounced all personal property and self-will; everything they did was at the motion of the prelate's nod. Their discipline balanced manual labour, private contemplation, and the choir service. It repudiated art and learning, both being considered detrimental to the spiritual life, a distraction from it, and an irrelevance. This spirit is reflected in their architecture of the first half of the twelfth century. Whereas most churches, whether parish, cathedral or monastic, were adorned with painted statues in niche and buttress, and resplendent in painted plaster surfaces within and without, and illuminated by stained-glass windows, hanging lamps and candle-sticks of decorative wrought-iron, 'great trees of brass, fashioned with wondrous skill, all aglitter with jewels as much as with candlelight', the early Cistercians would have none of these things. White plaster only was permitted. Crossing towers were forbidden, save only of the lowest height. There were to be no bell-towers, no coloured glass.

Thus their builders perforce made the most of basic forms without the adventitious aids of surface decoration. And right well they did it. Clear glass permitted small windows. White-washed walls prevailed. The austere beauty of the finest Cistercian abbeys is a true reflection of their spiritual ideals and the life which was followed in them. The ideals were not followed absolutely. There are Cistercian crossing-towers, and bell-towers, and sculptured capitals, even in early works. But, on the whole, Cistercian architecture of the twelfth century and early thirteenth century is characteristically plain. In Scotland it always is. From the second half of the thirteenth century, however, a gradual liberation from restriction is apparent.

The fulminations of St Bernard against artistic endeavour are well-known. He said 'Sacred images form the pavement that we walk on: here one spits on the face of an angel, there the features of a saint are effaced by the feet of the passers-by . . . to what purpose are these ridiculous monsters, this deformed beauty and beautiful deformity . . .?' Another, in conceding that some churches may be painted, provided the painting is instructive, nevertheless attacked vain expense in decoration.

Twelfth-century art was primarily a monastic art and it was against the flourishing art of the Benedictines that such observations were directed, for it was under the abbots St Hugh and Peter the Venerable of Cluny that sculpture was reborn in France in the eleventh century. The Benedictines did not think that art was dangerous. When the Cistercian St Bernard was stripping churches of ornament the Benedictines were encouraging it, in elaborate sculptural pieces for doorways, and rich mouldings for minor details.

As the Cistercians aimed to achieve complete self-sufficiency, to be independent of the world outside, they sought remote and difficult country for their houses.[1] Benefactors are known to have extirpated villages and the monks to have depopulated the countryside to ensure the desired solitude. The labour involved in the self-imposed struggle for existence created a need for lay-brothers, *conversi*, to perform duties too distracting for the choir monk. They were fully part of the monastic family, and they became so numerous and important in the Cistercian order that they were provided with their own cloisters and domestic ranges, and used the nave of the abbey church as their own choir. The consequent exclusion of the public from

[1] '*In civitatibus, castellis, villis, nulla nostra construenda sunt coenobia, sed in locis a conversatione hominum semotis.*'

that part of the church which could be, and often was,
available for parochial services led to the provision of public
chapels near the gate.

The first Cistercian house in England was Waverley, in
Surrey, founded in 1128-9 but the harsh environment of the
north of England offered a challenge more to their liking.
Here was a territory not yet recovered from the systematic
devastation by which Duke William had solved a problem.
From Rievaulx in Yorkshire first settled in 1131, a colony
went to Scotland five years later. Here as elsewhere the
family multiplied with remarkable fecundity. There were
eleven full abbeys and a number of dependent houses, and
they spread as far as Kinloss in Moray.

The Augustinian and Premonstratensian
Canons Regular

The great Benedictine orders, whether of Cluny or of the
reforming movements, were for cloistered monks whose duty
lay not with the world outside. Although the planting of
Cluniac houses along the pilgrim routes, to the shrines of
St Peter at Rome and St James (Santiago) at Compostella
in Spain, was both profitable and meritorious, and although
the dispensing of alms and hospitality was likewise for the
common good, the needs of church as a whole were not met
by these monasteries, nor were they intended to be. The
cloistered monk, even when in priestly orders, did not
administer to the cure of souls nor perform the services of
baptism, marriage and burial. There consequently arose, to
remedy this shortcoming in the monastic system and to
provide a service useful to the secular church, the Augustinians and the Premonstratensians, whose constitutions did
not prohibit extra-cloistral activities but made specific provision for them. The Augustinians lived in community,
followed a strict rule based upon that of St Augustine of
Hippo (ob. 430) renounced personal possessions and were
celibate; but they went out, and they preached. Similar
to the Augustinian in origin and purpose but of greater

strictness was the order of Prémontré, whose members were known as 'white canons', from the colour of their habit, as the Augustinians were known as 'black canons' from the colour of their habit.

The manner in which the Premonstratensian order was founded is characteristic, and demonstrates not only the manner in which an order could be founded but the doubt which almost always attends a foundation date, usually given with finality, and indeed so given throughout this book.

The order was founded by St Norbert, a high-born ascetic who was attached to the court of the archbishop of Cologne in the early years of the twelfth century. Norbert had little interest in the religious life, although connected with it, until he experienced a disillusionment in Rome. His conversion was accomplished when he was thrown from his horse in a thunderstorm. He retired to a Benedictine abbey and subsequently earned clerical displeasure by attempting to reform the canons of a church to which he was connected as a subdeacon. He therefore withdrew from it, sold all his possessions, and gave his money to the poor. Barefoot he made his way to the pope for protection and guidance. Fortified with a licence to preach he undertook an evangelising mission with three companions. They died, overcome by the hardship they endured. Although encouraged by the bishop of Laon, a supporter of monastic reform, Norbert nevertheless failed to gather recruits. He settled *c* 1120 in a ruined chapel which was presented to him by Benedictine monks. Then a community gathered about him, and a constitution or rule of conduct and behaviour became necessary. After seeking advice he chose the Augustinian rule as the basis of his house, for he had a call to preach widely to monastic and clerical audiences and to the people at large as well as a desire to follow a life of austerity and contemplation such as only a monastery could provide. The Premonstratensians expanded rapidly in France, and it became necessary to revise the rule of St Augustine and to clarify the position of the mother-house at Prémontré in its relation to its daughter-houses. Accordingly *c* 1130 further constitutions were drawn up. The order was pre-eminently indebted to Cîteaux, from whom it borrowed freely in framing regulations governing its organisation and constitution and in its admission of lay-brothers, although they were not so numerous as they were in Cistercian houses. Accordingly, the Premonstratensian order became an ingenious blend of the Benedictine, the reformed Benedictine and the Augustinian—of the contemplative and the active aspects of twelfth-century monasticism. This duality is expressed in the generic name which the Premonstratensian shared with the Augustinian. As opposed to 'monks' they were known as 'canons regular' *ie* canons who lived according to a rule (*regulus*). In a real sense the two orders of canons regular were the successors of the monks and the precursors of the preaching friars.

Only a few Cistercian and Benedictine houses were founded in the second half of the twelfth century, at which time nearly all the English and Scottish Premonstratensian houses were created. The secluded monks had had their day, and the shift of enthusiasm from the contemplative to the missionary and preaching life achieved its sweeping triumph with the introduction of the new orders of preaching friars, the Dominicans and the Franciscans, about the middle of the thirteenth century. No great difference between monks and canons regular was made by the generality of people at the time. To the mediaeval laymen the distinction was one of origin rather than of fact. They were apparently the same, as were the buildings they created. The only sizeable Premonstratensian house in Scotland is Dryburgh abbey, and there is nothing distinctively Premonstratensian about it. The Augustinians were better represented, as the following pages will show. Their houses were among the largest, and their influence in ecclesiastical and secular affairs was considerable.

There were, then, two main streams in the current of twelfth century monasticism, each in a distinctive way stressing its two opposite aspects, the worldly and the other-worldly, which had afforded matter for dispute since early Christian times. These are matters of historical importance, but they affect architecture only in a general way. The visitor to any monastic site in Scotland will be hard put to identify the order to which it belonged.

The architecture of our abbeys was truly European. Not until the widespread creation of collegiate churches in the fifteenth century do we have a national ecclesiastical architecture. The great Benedictine orders, the Cluniacs especially, appealed to the pilgrim traffic by building on its routes and by providing numerous shrines and altars in the pilgrim churches for the edification and veneration of the devout, and such churches assumed more complicated plans thereby. Cistercian churches on the other hand, made no such concessions to public admittance and participation in the religious services held within them, by reason of the order's seclusion and greater stress on severity, which alone would have been inimical to lay enthusiasm had such a thing been desired. The Cistercian east end, not being provided with an elaboration of altars, nor with ambulatories for the circulation of pilgrims to numerous shrines, was extremely simple, but it was in fact adopted by other orders in the later twelfth century, so that even this architectural expression of Cistercian principles cannot be taken as an identifying characteristic. In any event the Cistercians underwent fundamental changes, as have been described above, and the trend to soften austerity in observances was reflected in the architecture of later building periods which show a freer use of decorative effects than one would expect who had only the original ideals in mind. In England and France where a greater number of buildings of the earliest periods survives and where the total number of all periods is much greater than there ever was in Scotland, it is possible to study architectural development and decline. This is not so in Scotland. Consequently our description of monastic architecture is comprehensive and in general terms.

The Buildings

The monastery is the home of a spiritual family. Like all families the conventual one has its domestic aspect. Monastic buildings reflect the double nature of the conventual life. The heart and soul of the church was the high altar, the dwelling-place of the convent was the cloister which usually lies on the south and sunny side of the church, in the angle formed by the nave and the south transept. Round it were four covered walks or alleys. Properly speaking these were the cloisters. As well as providing ample space for contemplative activities such as reading and instruction they afforded easy and direct access to the ranges of buildings which enclosed the open cloister court. The normal arrangement (fig. 1) of these buildings was similar in all houses, of all orders, and at all periods, with the notable exception of the houses of the Carthusian order whose exceptional emphasis on the private rather than the communal life required a series of cells and small walled gardens round the cloisters. There are of course exceptions to the standard Benedictine plan from which all houses derived their variations, but these are usually due to local circumstances and conditions of site and drainage. The greatest variation to be found is in the placing of the cloister and domestic buildings on the north side of the church. This was invariably for water-supply, as at Melrose (fig. 2).

The cloisters were covered by a lean-to roof falling from the walls of the surrounding buildings to an open arcade looking into the cloister court. At the east end of the north cloister, in the south wall of the church, is the east processional doorway through which the monks passed from the

church on great processions. At the west end of the same
wall is the west processional doorway by which they returned to the church. In some Cistercian houses the west
processional doorway is not in the cloisters but at the north
end of the west range; in others re-entry to the nave was
through the great west doorway in the west front of the
church.

The west range of the cloisters might be called the secular
part of the monastery. Before it lay the great court and the
gatehouse. It confronted the outer world. It was at the
disposal of the cellarer, the monk responsible for the provis-
ioning of the convent with victuals and all material requirements. He was the convent's chief link with the outside
world, frequently absent at the monasteries' granges, and
at fairs and markets, buying and selling and consequently
exempt from much of the exacting choir services. He was
to avoid the habit of 'trafficking like a tradesman, of striving
too eagerly after slender profit, or of driving a hard bargain
from those who could ill afford it'. From him the monks
could obtain the little extra for the entertainment of their
relatives and friends, or the small tokens of affectionate remembrance, called *exennia*, which they were permitted to
send four times a year. The basement of the west range was
his store.

The almoner was here also 'his heart aglow with charity'.
He distributed the uneaten food which was collected in a
basket after every meal. And, when a monk died and a cross
was laid upon the table where he had sat and full meals had
been served at his place for thirty days, they were collected
and given by the almoner to the poor, that they might pray
for the soul of the departed brother.

Also in this range is the outer parlour where laymen were
received. Above or nearby are guest chambers, the respon-
sibility of the guest-master, who was enjoined to practise
religious hospitality as the rule of St Benedict would have
it *Hospites tamquam Christus suscipiantur*—Guests are to be
received as if they were Christ Himself. In houses containing

a great number of lay brothers, and in Cistercian houses particularly, the west range was appropriated for their use, with their frater or refectory on the ground floor and dorter (dormitory) above, which more or less echoed the arrangements for the choir monks on the east side of the cloister. Where lay-brothers were numerous the west range extends to great length beyond the south range.

The east range of the cloister is an extension from the transept. Its abutment against the transept gable afforded an opportunity and a challenge to the designer for interesting improvisation in fenestration. At Dryburgh, for example, a series of narrow lancets steps up each roof slope; at Sweetheart, the roof of the east range encroaches into a large circular window which is appropriately adjusted to receive it; at Arbroath, lancets of different size are asymmetrically placed to clear the roof. Although this range is an extension of the church it is a quite distinct building, a part of the cloister, not a part of the church to which it is so effectively attached. The church, although clasping and overshadowing, is a thing apart. The only direct communication from church to east range on the first floor is from the dorter to the transept by the night stairs. On the ground floor a door in the middle of the transept gable admits to the chamber which lies immediately alongside the transept gable. This was usually divided by a cross-wall into two parts, the east part being the sacristy which was entered from the transept, the west part being the library or book cupboard, accessible only from the cloister alley. The next chamber away from the church is the inner parlour, where some conversation was permitted; next to this, in the middle of the east range, is the chapter-house, with a fine doorway flanked by arched openings as befitted its importance. It was so called because at the daily meeting of the convent which was held in it a chapter of the rule (not the bible) was read, and the martyrology, and the names of benefactors and distinguished dead who were due for remembrance. Obits, obituary rolls, or bede-rolls which had perchance arrived by messengers, (breviators), were noted for the abbey's own record and brought up to date if necessary before continuing on their way to other monasteries with requests for prayers for the soul of the deceased, who might be monk or layman. Other solemnities took place in the chapter-house, which frequently projects to the east for greater room and dignity.

Next to it is the day stair, so called because of its use in daytime for access to the dorter which overran the whole of the first floor. An alternative position for the stair is further down the east range, or at the east end of the south range. The east range continues beyond the south range of the cloister to finish usually with the reredorter or latrine block, beneath which flowed a great drain. The reredorter block projects usually eastwards at right-angles to the east range, not always from the end of it. At Melrose, for example, it is about half-way, close to and parallel with the projecting chapter-house. The site was determined by the availability of running water to flush the latrine pits.

Considerable ingenuity was exercised in the provision of monastic sanitation. Monastic great drains or conduits were of no mean size, as we shall see at Melrose and St Andrews. They were well built and not infrequently formed a long water-course diverting the required water from a source some hundreds of yards away. The conduit at St Andrews cathedral-priory must be about half-a-mile long, tapping the Kinness Burn, passing under the reredorter and returning to the burn where the harbour now is. It has been traced in the middle of the town, among houses, gardens and roads. The reredorter drain is the true but unromantic explanation of the mysterious subterranean passages which are improbably supposed to have been of some service to monks.

The south range is primarily that of the frater, or refectory, with a kitchen on one side of it and perhaps the warming-house (the common-room), on the other. The kitchen lies at the west end of the frater. It thus served the choir monks' frater and the lay brothers' frater in the west range. In early Cistercian houses the frater was placed parallel to the cloister walk, occupying almost all of it, but towards the end of the twelfth century it was turned at right angles to the cloister walk and projected far to the south. This gained space for the warming-house and kitchen on either side of it.

The monastic day began about midnight. Then the monks arose from their beds in the dorter, passed through the night stair doorway, down the night stairs in the south transept, and so to their appointed positions in the choir for the first office of the day. A similar arrangement in the west range permitted the lay brothers to descend from their dorter to the nave of the church which was their choir.

In a cruciform church (there is no symbolic significance in the shape[1]) the nave is the main part extending from the west end to the transepts. Advancing to the east from them is the eastern limb of the cross, generally referred to as the choir, consisting of the ritual choir, the presbytery and the sanctuary, where the high altar stood. It should be noted that the ritual choir, which contained the monks' stalls, very frequently extended westwards into the crossing and even encroached into the architectural nave (figs. 1, 2). This is due to the Cistercian short east end, which was so popular with monastic planners in Britain and which prevailed in Scotland. It does not occur in cathedral and collegiate churches. In them the choir was of sufficient length to accommodate the requisite number of canons' stalls, which number was in any case less likely to be variable than was the case in monastic communities. The monastic choir was separated from the nave by a massive stone screen, known as the pulpitum screen, which had a doorway in the middle,

[1] The transepts, or 'cross-church' as they are sometimes called, were derived from the primitive 'porticus' of early Saxon churches. This was not a porch in the modern sense of vestibule, but an annexe attached to the church and entered only from within it. The porticus contained an altar and was used as the burial-place of dignitaries. There was frequently a porticus on the north and south walls, and from them the transepts developed.

with a nave altar on either side of it. Three survive in Scotland: Glasgow Cathedral has a magnificent complete pulpitum, Melrose and Lincluden (Dumfries) possess good if somewhat battered examples.

In addition to the high altar, there were chapels in the transepts which had evolved in response to the need for more altars. And in addition to them there were side chapels in the nave and choir aisles. These were separated one from another and from the main parts by stone or timber screens. The altars they contained were served by the minority of monks who were in priestly orders, and they were founded and endowed by individual or corporate benefactors and dedicated to a saint favoured by the founder. The trade and craft guilds founded altars for perpetual masses—the hammer-men in honour of their patron St Eloi (Eloy), the baxters (bakers) in honour of St Aubert (Obert, Towbert, Cobort) and so on.

Essential buildings not connected with the disciplined life of the cloister lie to the south and east. Their situation is more liable to variation. Nonetheless there is general conformity. The cemetery is most frequently east of the east range, and reached by a passage through it. To the south of the cemetery, in the south-eastern part of the monastery, the infirmary and its chapel are to be expected. They are strictly conventual buildings. But the guest-house is not, and if not in the west range, is to be expected somewhere near it with the gatehouse nearby.

Away from the services of the church and the seclusion of the cloisters the secular buildings of a monastery attracted daily and frequent contact with the lay world outside the monastic precincts. To and from the guest-house, the lay infirmary, the bakehouse, stables, workshops and masons' yards a constant traffic of wheeled vehicles, horses and pedestrians passed into the monastery. It was the purpose of the gatehouse to control such traffic and to defend the entrance, and as the monastic builder did not lose the opportunity thus provided to impress upon the beholder a true sense of the Church's secular power and authority, the gatehouse of a monastery invariably presents an imposing example of secular architecture not entirely innocent of businesslike preparations for defence. Gatehouses in England are numerous, but not in Scotland. In fact only two, at St Andrews and Arbroath, have by good fortune come down to us. A gatehouse is basically a vaulted passage sufficiently provided with heavy doors and a portcullis which was operated from a porter's lodgings above the vault. At Arbroath and St Andrews a gatehouse such as this exists in equal completeness. At the former, ranges of imposing vaulted buildings extend from the gatehouse, to make the gatehouse range of Arbroath one of the finest in Britain.

Precinct walls are likewise rare, having been far-flung and vulnerable to demolition. St Andrews has however a splendid and almost complete circuit, fortified by towers, and of good height. Sweetheart is enclosed by a mantle wall of remarkable cyclopean masonry and at Pluscarden much of the wall remains.

The more one studies the monastic plan the more does one marvel at its sheer efficiency. Innumerable conflicting requirements are successfully met and resolved with such ease that they are altogether unsuspected. The requirements of quiet and of conversation, contemplation and activity, sleeping and eating, cooking, provisions, the round of liturgical services, admission and segregation of the laity, and the simple but frequently baffling problem of how to enable people to move from one part to another with the minimum of effort and disturbance were fulfilled to the satisfaction of all with the utmost economy of means and exertion. It is simple; it is straightforward, and it works. It is logical; it expresses the functions of the buildings and their relative importance. The spiritual centre of gravity of a monastery is in the east, and there we have the weight of building. It is little wonder that it scarcely altered in four hundred and fifty years of mediaeval monasticism. We are reminded of the architect of our own time, to whom reference has already been made,[1] who was repeatedly brought back to the mediaeval solution of his problems. And furthermore, the plan looks good on paper, as a pattern, as all good plans do.

[1] See above, p. 2.

The Monastic Orders in Scotland

The rapid expansion of fully developed European monasticism in Scotland in the twelfth century was not a revival of an older Benedictine form which had fortunately survived the destructive onslaughts of the barbarian invaders in the Dark Ages. It was a transformation.

When Margaret, born and brought up in Hungary, the daughter of an exiled Saxon prince, married Malcolm Canmore *c* 1070, monasticism in Scotland, as much as it can be said to have existed, was Celtic. To Scotland, at Dunfermline where she had been married, she introduced for the first time the Benedictine conventual discipline. She thus initiated a long and continuous royal encouragement of the religious life, and particularly the monastic aspect of it which was its most distinctive mediaeval characteristic. The exact date of the founding of Holy Trinity or Christ's Church, Dunfermline, as a daughter-house of Holy Trinity or Christ's Church, Canterbury, is unknown, but that it was due to the efforts of Margaret and the co-operation of Archbishop Lanfranc is clear from a charter of her son David I, *c* 1128, which names nearly all of the royal family as benefactors.

Margaret had six sons. All shared in what has been justly called a family enterprise. It was indeed the exclusive work of the royal house. Edgar, who first succeeded her, resumed early connections with Durham. These had been less successful than the Canterbury innovation, although the prior of Durham had been Margaret's spiritual adviser as well as her biographer. Edgar's effort was successful. A gift to Durham of land at Coldingham *c* 1098 led to the founding of a dependent cell there, probably at first a grange or manor for the supervision of Durham lands on the Scottish side of the border, but by 1139 or 1140 a regular monastery served by Durham monks. Coldingham is frequently attributed to Edgar as a foundation of his. This is doubtful, but the gift is not, and Coldingham priory grew from it.

Both Dunfermline and Coldingham were of the strongest Benedictine antecedants. Alexander I favoured the Augustinian canons regular at an early date, and introduced them to Scone *c*1120, only some ten years after their arrival in England from France. Of the monastery of Scone nothing of the structure remains—except perhaps the Stone of Destiny in Westminster Abbey, which looks uncommonly like a thirteenth-century building-stone, and could be, were Edward I deceived when he pillaged the abbey and sought that strange palladium of the Scottish race. Scone was colonised by canons from St Oswald's priory at Nostell in Yorkshire. From Scone the Augustinians colonised the new cathedral-priory of St Andrews, with the prior of Scone as its first bishop and a canon of Scone as its prior. The significance of this strong Augustinian penetration from Yorkshire to St Andrews, by way of Scone, is re-inforced by the unique and splendid St Regulus' church adjacent to the cathedral. It bears striking similarities to the contemporary church of Wharram-le-Street, a cell of Nostell priory.

With the rise of power and influence of David, the sixth son of Margaret, as earl of Huntingdon from 1114-24 and as king from 1124 to his death in 1153, the monastic movement accelerates with remarkable rapidity and completeness. David was founder and patron of a wide variety of religious orders and early proved himself uncommonly receptive to the religious forces at work. He seems to have had a special regard for abbot St Bernard and his Tironensians, with whose name and reputation he had doubtless become familiar during his years at the Court of his brother-in-law, Henry I, who was himself a patron of the order and had visited Tiron. David earnestly requested Bernard to send

monks to Scotland. These he endowed with land by the
Tweed and settled at Selkirk *c* 1113, only four years after
the original foundation in the forest near Chartres. Some
time later he travelled to Tiron to see Bernard, but failed to
arrive before the saint's death in 1116 or 1117. He returned
to Selkirk with a further twelve monks and an abbot. In
1128 they moved to Kelso, to a more suitable site than was
apparently available to them at Selkirk.

The order of Tiron claims a special place in Scottish
monastic history. South of the border it is represented by
only an abbey and dependencies, but in Scotland no less
than four major houses were founded in the twelfth century,
and each was of pre-eminent architectural merit, and there
was a number of dependencies besides. Furthermore, the
settlement at Selkirk was the first footing of the order in
Britain, and not only to Selkirk but to Kilwinning also the
convents came from France.

In 1136 Bishop John of Glasgow sought refuge from papal
displeasure at Tiron but was recalled to Scotland two years
later. He assisted David 1 in founding Jedburgh abbey, a
house of Augustinian canons, first mentioned as a priory
in 1139, and possibly founded to signalise the bishop's re-
conciliation with the papacy the year before. Bishop John
was buried in Jedburgh in 1147, and shortly afterwards the
monastery was promoted to abbatial status. A contemporary recorded that David founded a house for canons of
Beauvais, and by a process of elimination we conclude that
this was Jedburgh. Lacking proof the identity of Jedburgh's
mother-house must for the present remain uncertain, but it
seems to be very probable that Jedburgh was yet another
French colony.

The Augustinians played an important rôle in directing
the new currents of religious life to the north. In England
they possessed over two hundred houses. None held key
positions, but in Scotland their supremacy was unchallenged
with Jedburgh, Holyrood, St Andrews and other houses to
be mentioned below. It is evidence of David's awareness of

the manifold influences of religious reform then affecting
church organisations throughout Europe that he encouraged
the Augustinians no less than the favoured Tironensians.
From Merton in Surrey he introduced them as the first
community of his new foundation of Holyrood in 1128. To
Stirling in 1140 he introduced French canons from Arrouaise, a particularly severe branch of the larger Augustinian
order, to found the monastery later known as Cambuskenneth.

The Premonstratensians did not appear upon the rapidly
expanding monastic scene until 1152, the year before
David's death, when Hugh de Moreville's foundation of
1150 was established at Dryburgh by monks from Alnwick.
Save for Dryburgh the Premonstratensians do not figure
conspicuously among our monastic sites, but Whithorn is
of outstanding historical importance and can justly claim to
be the church site with the longest continuous history in
Britain, for it has the east end of St Ninian's church, the
Premonstratensian cathedral-priory upon it, and upon the
ruins of that there stands the parish church of today.

David founded no Premonstratensian houses, but the
royal patronage was none the less comprehensive and
embraced all aspects and attitudes of mediaeval monasticism. To the Benedictine establishments of the older
discipline at Dunfermline and Coldingham he added,
shortly before his death, a Cluniac priory on the lonely Isle
of May in the Firth of Forth. It became neither prosperous
nor powerful, nor did it break the firm allegiance exacted
by Cluniac parenthood, but its ruins represent matter of
abiding interest, for this island monastery served monks
who came from as far away as Reading to tend the shrine
of a Celtic saint.

The first Cistercian convent in Scotland came from
Rievaulx in Yorkshire in 1136. Two years previously that
abbey had received the saintly Ailred into the habit. He had
been brought up under David's patronage as companion to
his son Henry and his stepson Waldef, was highly esteemed

by the king, and eventually held office in the household. It was upon the king's business that he passed near the abbey of Rievaulx where he was converted. Waldef too renounced the Court for the habit, and became prior of the Augustinian Kirkham. He renounced this also, to become a novice at Rievaulx (much to the Augustinians' displeasure)[1] and eventually became abbot of Melrose in 1148. In the previous year Ailred had been elected abbot of Rievaulx. There was thus an intimate connection between the Scottish Court and the very vanguard of the Cistercian advance.

Of the two militant orders, the Knights Templars and the Knights Hospitallers, little can be said. Fortunately something substantial can be seen, at Torpichen, the only certain house of Hospitallers of St John in Scotland. Much remains of it, albeit not all of the twelfth century. The transepts of its church and the crossing between them are remarkably complete, and like most of the other monastic monuments referred to are in the custody of the Ministry. This house is alleged to have been founded by David, but there is no proof of this.

Monasticism was the ideal form of the religious life in the Middle Ages. To contemporaries its swift and widespread development in Scotland was David's main achievement. Yet at his death in 1153 it had by no means reached its furthest expansion. Many other houses were yet to be established, some as daughter-houses of his own foundations. Every new monastery in Scotland was another symbol of the Norman Conquest, another link with France. Craftsmen followed in the wake of the monks—or preceded them—to

[1] Change from one order to another was unpopular and permissible only by special dispensation as contrary to the vow of stability which bound a monk to his order for life. When the celebrated Adam of Dryburgh left that house for the Carthusian Witham there was much Premonstratensian resentment, and renowned as he was for his Premonstratensian writings and reputation his name does not appear in the necrology of that order. The Carthusian appeal was limited, because of its unbending severity, but it had an attraction for committed monks who were yet unsatisfied.

erect their churches and cloisters not always in the native
style, as John Moreau's testament proclaims in Melrose.
These men fortified the Norman element and owed much
to the patronage of Scotland's French-speaking aristocracy.

Due to their parochial responsibilities the Augustinian
and Premonstratensian canons frequently settled where an
earlier church was or had been. A Celtic church might
be expected at a house of canons regular. Benedictine,
including Cluniac and Tironensian houses, are less likely to
succeed earlier churches, but might do so. Cistercian houses
are not at all likely to be over or beside earlier churches, for
parochial duties and responsibilities had no part in Cistercian life. Their houses were erected on virgin sites, far
from the abodes of men (pp. 36, 55-6).

The Ancient Monuments[1]

The following brief descriptions are primarily intended for
visitors and intending visitors to the monastic ruins of
Scotland which are in the care of the Ministry of Public
Building and Works.

They are noble works of architecture at their best, in
the full floodstream of European achievement at a great
creative epoch in which Scotland played her part, when the
issue of gothic out of romanesque architecture was one of the
most dramatic episodes in the history of European art. All
our abbeys belong to this period, and to those who approach
them observantly (Ruskin said that one cathedral looked
very like another if viewed with the eyes shut) the transition
is obvious, either by forceful comparisons in the one building,
in the astounding contrast of the choir of Jedburgh with the
nave of a later generation, for example, or in different
buildings, such as Dunfermline and Kelso, which present
their sturdy romanesque for comparison with Dundrennan's
early gothic. The deep devotional and contemplative in-
stinct is expressed in bold and vigorous terms in all of them
and we would do well in contemplating their ruins to
recollect that we are in the presence of an authentic part of
the Middle Ages.

The scenic beauty and rural peace of our abbeys pro-
vokes comment on how those old monks knew a thing or
two about how to make life pleasant for themselves, and
does injustice to the monks thereby. This is to view the

[1] Unless otherwise stated the sites described are Ancient Monuments
in the Ministry's care. Most of them are: see county list, pp. 95-96.

monasteries through twentieth-century eyes momentarily released from urban turbulence. Far from seeking pleasant places the monks sought the challenge of hardship and tribulation. The reformed orders were created because the established orders were not hard enough. The Cistercians regarded themselves as voices crying in the wilderness, to save their souls. All they sought was waste, water, and trees. Hence the number of their houses in the wild and un-populated hills and dales of Yorkshire and in the uneasy and troubled frontier between England and Scotland. The monks did not withdraw from their friends and relatives to make a silent world in a walled enclosure, to fast and pray and suffer in penance in order to enjoy the scenery. There was plenty of scenery.

There is less today, and as the beauty of architecture and a just appreciation of it, the effect it has upon the mind of the beholder, extends to and is influenced by its situation and environment, our abbeys are set off to their fullest scenic advantage. The ruins are preserved and laid out for the pleasure and instruction of the public according to the terms and intentions of the Ancient Monuments Acts. They are in every sense public buildings, and the public good is ever in the minds of those who have the privilege of tending to their care and maintenance.

They have suffered some grievous blows in their day. The blame has been laid at the door of zeal and reform of a different sort. It is no part of the purpose of this book to discuss alleged Protestant destruction, but one observation is justified, for it arises from the evidence of the architecture. In almost every case the north wall of the monastic church has comprehensively vanished, while the south wall remains high and of full length. This cannot be explained away as coincidence. It occurs too often for that; at Arbroath, Jedburgh, St Andrews, Dryburgh, Glenluce, Sweetheart and Kilwinning; and at Dundrennan also, although less striking, the disparity is there.

When the monks were no longer simply 'the religious'

but Roman Catholics, when the abbey churches were Catholic churches, their day was done. For the Protestant faith new churches were usually erected. The mediaeval church was redundant, its walls expendable, and the north wall the most accessible. But the south wall confronted an open cloister court, a useful garden, and it afforded for that garden a high protective north wall with an uninterrupted southern exposure. It could be put to use, and thus it has survived.[1]

If this thesis is correct, it throws some light upon the alleged depredations of the Reformation. It indicates that the present ruination is the result of neglect and neighbourly stone-quarrying. And what would be more natural, with roofs collapsed and the great edifices in rapid decline, with no future save what legislation would provide more than three hundred years later? There is much evidence to support this explanation. Houses and gardens in the neighbourhood of abbeys yield quantities of carved mediaeval stones, corbels, vault-bosses, capitals and bases, moulded shaft and arch stones and the like, in great number, while infinitely more building stones, recognisable only by the expert eye, have gone to the making of post-Reformation buildings. More will be recovered as these buildings are demolished. Only recently a substantial fragment of a recumbent effigy of a bishop was recovered in alterations to a house in St Andrews. It had been split lengthways to serve as a window lintel.[2] The site museums at St Andrews and Melrose contain many stones from neighbouring buildings and garden walls of considerable age. Stone-robbing explains also the unsightly 'lumpes of Walls and heapes of stones' which disfigure so many of our abbeys.

---

[1] It is likely to be the earliest and longest-lived portion of the nave; first up, last down. Building in height began with the eastern limbs. When they were ready for use (not infrequently under a temporary roof) the nave was begun, the south wall first, to support the roof of the north cloister, which would at this stage probably serve temporary cloister buildings.

[2] It is now in the St Andrews cathedral site museum.

SA E

The good ashlar faces have been removed for use elsewhere, to leave the formless core exposed.

BENEDICTINE HOUSES

Dunfermline Abbey, Fife

Christ Church, Dunfermline, was founded by Margaret *c* 1074 as a daughter-house of Christ Church, Canterbury, the mother-church of the Christian faith in England. From Canterbury Archbishop Lanfranc sent monks for this historic adventure. The monks were few, the church was small, and the convent probably did not survive the anti-foreign national resistance of Donald Ban after the death of Malcolm and Margaret in 1093. The remains of an early church have been recovered beneath the nave of the great romanesque church which superseded it, and they are of much importance. They represent two distinct but connected building operations, each of unusual interest. To a small pre-Conquest church, consisting of an oblong cell with a square western tower, there was added on the east a square choir with a rounded apse. The earlier belongs to a tenth-eleventh century type of manorial or in this instance palace church, and was doubtless that in which Margaret was married: the addition, with its characteristically romanesque apse, may be attributed to Margaret and thus signalises the introduction of the romanesque style to Scotland.

The plan of the early church is indicated on the paving of the nave of the existing church which was begun in the reign of her son, David I, *c* 1128, and which was dedicated in 1150. It is important to know what stage in the great twelfth-century church this dedication commemorates. We do not know. There would be two dedications; one for the completion of the eastern limbs, which would then be put to use; the other for the completion of the whole work, which might be some twenty years later if all went well. If 1150 is the date of the second dedication it includes the completed nave, if it is of the first dedication it throws the nave into the second half of the twelfth century.

Marked stylistic mannerisms in the treatment of the nave arcade, particularly the bold incised ornamentation of the piers, connect it with Durham, which was nearing completion in 1128, the year the new and larger church at Dunfermline was begun, when the priory was raised to abbatial status. Although completion by 1150 of a church whose magnitude is indicated by the surviving nave means sustained and energetic building not by any means characteristic of the times, the continuing interest and benefactions of the royal house of Canmore could explain it, particularly as it became the royal sepulchre of succeeding generations, with Margaret herself being buried there, first in her own church then in her son's. The triforium is of primitive type, argues for the earlier date, and supports the stylistic connections with the Benedictine Durham.

The east end and transepts are entirely demolished. They were replaced in the nineteenth century by a church which is still in use, but the nave has survived mercifully unaltered in the main (Pl. 2). All things considered it is the finest romanesque interior in Scotland. It is rivalled only by St Magnus' Cathedral in Kirkwall, which has a thirteenth-century vault over a contemporary clerestory.

The Dunfermline west front, with lofty side towers flanking a narrow pedimented gable, flat and without buttresses or sculpture, irresistibly recalls early romanesque or even Carolingian façades. Seen from a distance (Pl. 1) it is one of our most striking elevations. It is, in fact, a late composition incorporating the original west door. This is a distinguished feature in five recessed and richly decorated orders with round and octagonal side shafts, a notable example of old work sympathetically handled by later masons one of whom was William Schaw, Master of Works to James VI. He erected the north-west tower and an extension to the north porch in 1594, both good examples of late mediaeval Scots gothic.

It is appropriate to mention here that the north porch of the nave of a monastic church to which the laity was admitted was by way of being a civic porch. Here civil ceremonies such as marriage were celebrated, the public payment of debts transacted, and such other solemnities as required witnesses were performed. In the absence and infrequency of written records of such matters public witness was essential, and among those present were children whose evidence would last longest. Chaucer's Wife of Bath—'Husbondes at the chirche dore hadde she fyve'— did not desert them there. She married them at the church door, probably the door of the north porch, the 'marriage porch' as it is sometimes called. The notice boards to be seen in church porches today are reminders of the times when churches and churchyards were places of public meetings and information.

Nothing of the east and west sides of Dunfermline's cloister remains, but the frater, rising high from its under-crofts on a level much lower than the cloister presents to the south a splendid thirteenth-century façade. There was a royal residence close to the abbey since the early twelfth century, probably since the marriage of Malcolm and Margaret. The remains of a palace whose masonry dates from the thirteenth century are connected to the abbey cloister by a vaulted gatehouse. They tower sixty feet high over a ravine in the adjacent public park, and from there the palace is best seen. It continued to be a principal residence of the Scottish kings until the seventeenth century. Charles I was born in it in 1600 but after the reign of Charles II it fell into ruin and was thereafter neglected until placed in the custody of the Office (Ministry) of Works.

Other Benedictine houses of which some remains exist and which are not in the custody of the Ministry of Public Building and Works are: Iona abbey, 1203, (restored); Isle of May priory *c* 1150 (of Cluniac origin[1]); Pluscarden,

[1] See above, p. 34.

originally a Valliscaulian house, later absorbed into the Benedictine order[1]; and Coldingham priory.

Coldingham Priory, Berwickshire

Of a once extensive monastery (pp. 49-50) there remain only the north and east walls of the choir, parts of the south transept, and very fragmentary indications of the cloister buildings. The two surviving walls of the original long, unaisled choir (which has been restored for use) are unusually complete and lovely examples of late twelfth-early thirteenth-century work. Both internal and external elevations are treated in two equal storeys with much imagination, originality and refinement. On the outside the façades are in vertical bays separated by narrow pilaster buttresses, the lower storey with blind-arches; the upper with single lancets. The interior elevations (Pl. 3) are especially ingenious and lively exercises in pure lancet style with an uninterrupted horizontal emphasis. The lower range of wall-arcading is a swift repetition of simple moulded pointed arches with oval and quatrefoil recesses in the spandrels. In the open clerestory arcade immediately above it (there is no triforium) the pattern changes to an *a a b a a* rhythm, or one high open lancet, at each daylight opening, flanked by two subsidiary lancets. The variation is controlled by the long sequence of clustered shafts from which the arches spring. Each cluster is of the same height, the higher arches *b* being stilted upon diminutive shafts which rise from the same capitals as the flanking arches. The detailing of the capitals is somewhat crude in execution and pursues a new foliaceous inspiration with evident hesitation, but the conception of the whole, which owes its success to the way in which an unusually long wall surface has been exploited, is most sophisticated and without parallel in Scotland.

The building is in use for worship and is not in the Ministry's care.

[1] See below, p. 91.

CLUNIAC HOUSES

Paisley Abbey, Renfrewshire

Founded by Walter, son of Alan, steward of Scotland, *c*
1163. Colonised from Wenlock abbey, Shropshire. A
splendid example of late mediaeval ecclesiastical architecture in the grand manner. The original conventual buildings have been altered and absorbed in later work, but the
cloister court survives as a garden, the north and east alleys
have been restored, and the church continues in use. It
dates from a mid-fifteenth-century restoration, but includes
the original late twelfth-century east processional doorway,
and a thirteenth-century great west doorway in classic
lancet style. The aisled nave is complete and is distinguished
by a main arcade which is unusually graceful for this late
period, and a peculiar clerestory passage breaking out round
the alternate piers of the clerestory in corbelled projections
which overhang the nave (Pl. 4). An inordinately long choir
is unaisled and has a decorative sedilia. The well preserved
chapel of St Mirin projects eastwards from the vaulted
south transept. It contains a sculptured frieze, a notable and
all too rare example of Scottish interior sculpture, depicting scenes from the life of this Celtic saint who settled
here in the sixth century. The vault of this chapel repeats
a curiosity of construction paralleled in the presbytery of
Lincluden collegiate church in Dumfries, which is, a
double barrel-vault with false ribs applied to its under
surface in imitation of structural ribs. False ribs on barrel-
vaults are not uncommon in fifteenth-century ecclesiastical
work, but the double barrel-vault is most unusual and
indicates the secular influence of tower-house construction,
which is characterised by such vaults placed one upon
another. The abbey is in the centre of the city. It was
finally restored at the beginning of this century, and has two
fine windows by the late Douglas Strachan in the choir.
Being in use for worship the church is not in the Ministry's
care.

Crossraguel Abbey, Ayrshire

Founded by Duncan, Earl of Carrick, *c* 1214. At first an oratory, later an abbey dependent on Paisley. The first church was transeptal, but was destroyed, to be entirely rebuilt in its present form in the early fifteenth century with neither transept nor aisles. It is long and narrow, with frequent buttresses of bold projection. It is clearly influenced by the architecture of contemporary collegiate churches which were then coming into favour as the abbeys declined. The choir has a three-sided apse or chevet, one of the earliest examples in Scotland of this French type of east end.

The east range is particularly well preserved and contains two complete fifteenth-century rib-vaulted chambers of some interest, a sacristy and a chapter-house, in the position formerly occupied by the south transept. A late frater occupies the invariable position of this apartment in the south cloister range and doubtless stands upon the original frater. It contains the day stair to the dorter. Although ruined, the conventual buildings are well represented and extensive (Pl. 5) and include, in addition to those already mentioned, the foundations of the infirmary block. The reredorter drain is uncovered for inspection. It does not match those at Melrose and St Andrews but is none the less valuable for the very fact of its existence. There is a surprising tower-house of sixteenth-century date where the abbot's residence is to be expected, and the site is dominated by an even more surprising late mediaeval gate-house, also in thoroughly secular tower-house tradition.

May Island or Isle of May Priory, Fife: see pp. 34, 60.

TIRONENSIAN HOUSES

The architecture of the four great Tironensian abbeys is characterised by a powerful simplicity. The basic forms of arch and pier, wall, window and buttress, are handled with

a sure and bold sense of scale, which, as a common characteristic of a group, is altogether exceptional. As far as one
may generalise from a heritage of architecture which is
largely ruinous one may justly acknowledge a Tironensian
style.

Kelso Abbey, Roxburghshire

Founded first at Selkirk *c*1113 by David 1 when Earl of
Huntingdon; removed to Kelso 1128 in the third year of
his reign.[1] Nothing remains of the cloister buildings, but
what survives of the church is of surpassing interest as
one of the most spectacular achievements of romanesque
architecture in Scotland. It is comparable with the best
in England, and in some ways superior to Ely cathedral,
Cambridgeshire, to which it bears strong resemblances in
the handling of the west end, the only part of Kelso which
has survived. The remains consist of a western transept, a
high lantern tower over it, the adjacent bays of the nave and
half of the great west front and galilee porch. Western
transepts occur elsewhere in Scotland only at Kilwinning,
also a Tironensian abbey.

The internal elevations of the transept are arranged in
tiers of open arcaded galleries above a wall enriched with
intersecting arcading. This extremely effective composition
is to be compared with similar treatment in the transepts of
Arbroath, Peterborough, Norwich and Ely as outstanding
examples of the internal exploitation of the hollow or
galleried wall. The piers of the nave arcade are exceedingly
low and squat and the arches they carry are ponderous and
heavy. The triforium arcade on the other hand is rapid in
its movement and the main wall comes closely down behind
it, so that this also partakes of the hollow wall where there
is normally visible a dark void over the aisle vaults (Pl. 6).

The arcaded interiors contrast strongly with external
simplicity which is characteristically romanesque, with flat
pilaster buttresses of equal projection from top to bottom,

[1] See above, p. 51.

the various stages indicated by bold string courses, and the simplest of undecorated round arched windows, with corner shafts, pierce the thick walls. The external elevation of the north transept is particularly effective (Pl. 7). Advancing from its gable end is a pedimented porch containing a watching-chamber with five narrow lancet windows worked into a wall arcading of interlacing round arches. The gable of the porch is criss-crossed with a raised lattice pattern. Enough remains of the great western door of five recessed orders to indicate how richly sculptured it once was.

Kilwinning Abbey, Ayrshire

Founded by Hugh de Moreville *c* 1162. Little is known of its history, but what remains is first-rate architecture. A fine simple composition of three slender lancets in the gable wall of the south transept, and the piers and arches of the south transept chapels survive almost complete. The interior of the transept gable is treated somewhat more freely than the outside and is clearly the work of a sensitive designer. There is also an almost complete east processional doorway of exceeding refinement. Much of the south wall of the church survives, and enough of the west end to indicate a western transept, as at Kelso. The east range of the cloister survives in parts, with the chapter-house entrance flanked by two arched openings. The complete transept gable, its chapels, the processional doorway and the chapter-house doorway constitute an important assemblage of late twelfth- early thirteenth-century design, and the second occurrence of a western transept is of considerable importance in Scottish architectural history.

Arbroath Abbey, Angus

Founded by William the Lion in 1178 in honour of St Thomas Becket. Colonised from Kelso. The east end at least was completed by 1214, in which year the body of the founder was laid to rest beside the high altar. The abbot was consecrated in the year of foundation, *ie* presumably before the building was much advanced. The convent from Kelso evidently lived and worshipped perforce in timber buildings nearby while the great work went forward beside them. Much of the church remains in good height and the cloister foundations are extensive. A well preserved west front and south transept demonstrate the bold characteristics of Tironensian architecture (Pls. 8 and 10).

The deeply recessed west doorway is the most distinctively romanesque part of the abbey church. It derives enhanced architectural prominence from its position in an unusual barrel-vaulted projection whose purpose was to support an elevated tribune or galilee porch opening both to the inside and to the outside of the church; to the nave through six narrow pointed arches (Pl. 9), to the outside through three separate gablets which projected outwards some four feet from three arches in the main wall. The gablets were supported by two intermediate columns and at each end a solid stone haffit. The haffits remain, but the three gablets and the columns which supported them have now vanished, leaving exposed what was never meant to be seen. Midway between the interior arcade which overlooks the nave, and the present exterior arches, plain round columns with moulded capitals and bases support the lintels of the tribune passage which continues to the north tower. In Scotland there is evidence of two tribunes which may have served galilee porches, in the west fronts of St Andrews cathedral and Holyrood abbey, and the massive western porch at Kelso might also have been a galilee porch, but nothing like this tribune occurs anywhere else. In England, galilee porches are by no means common, and they are not as impressive as this.

The west front is flanked on either side by a massive tower open to the nave as an arch of the main arcading with an open triforium arch above (Pl. 9). The towers are unfloored and thus might have been conceived as western transepts, as at Kelso and Kilwinning. However, the designers at Arbroath chose not to have a lofty transeptal arch opening into the nave; they treated the internal wall of the tower as though the tower were floored. Consequently as well as the main arcade the triforium and clerestory arcades are carried across the inner wall of the tower, to convey an impression of triforium and clerestory where none in fact existed.

The south transept is a first-class piece of design, in large scale and noble simplicity. Immense lancet windows and an exceedingly large circular window in the pediment of the gable dominate the external elevations. The round window lit the roof space only, and was invisible from within the church. Its purpose was for design, and to lighten the load over the lancets beneath it. The internal wall surfaces are, like those at Kelso, enriched by galleries opening into the transepts, and beneath them the wall surfaces are treated as fields for sculpture, in the form of blind arcading, fashioned in round arches and pointed arches of different curvature upon clustered and single shafts (Pl. 10).

The lowest stages of the western towers were enriched by a fanciful and effective variation of this favourite romanesque motif of wall-arcading. The motif is developed a stage further than the orthodox continuous or intersecting series of arches. It is an arrangement of two arcades one above the other in a staggered setting, and the upper projects beyond, or overlaps, the lower. Consequently there is a sophisticated effect of movement, of projection and recession and rise and fall of the arches and shafts. A ghost of this mannerism lingers on the west face of the north tower: more is to be seen, with difficulty, upon the west face of the south tower, where it has been protected by the later gatehouse range. (Close examination is possible by undignified but commendable struggling through a garderobe or latrine chute in the east gable of the ground floor of this range).

The most complete and unaltered part of the church is a sacristy which was added to the south choir aisle between 1411 and 1499. It is a high vaulted apartment with lifeless and decadent detailing which is as characteristic of its time as the refinement and animation of the transept is typical of the late twelfth century. Contrived in one corner of the lofty sacristy is a raised treasury, for the safe-keeping of the abbey's riches, plate, sacramental vessels, muniments and so on. Access to this chamber, from the outside and from the sacristy also, was by ladder, a sound but unusual precaution.

The cloister ranges are totally demolished save for a vaulted undercroft connected to the kitchen at the west end of the south range. It is a fine late twelfth-century example of vaulted cellarage above which more important chambers were customarily erected. A later building, known as the Abbot's House, was erected upon it, which is now a site museum. The cloister ranges were extensive as their exposed foundations show, and include a kitchen court on the south side of the frater and kitchen range.

The abbey was completed in all its essentials *c* 1230 or thereby. At the end of the thirteenth century a large gate-house range was added to the south tower of the west façade of the church. It extends far in advance of the church over ground sloping down to the High Street of the town where it stops with a bulky square tower. A fortified gatehouse penetrates this range half-way along its length. It was vaulted in four bays and protected by gates and a portcullis operated in a room above the vaulted entrance-way. The precinct wall of the monastery, once of great extent but now entirely lost in urban development, swung in to meet the gatehouse at its inner end. The architecture of the gatehouse and its position in relation to the church and mantle wall have a close parallel in the contemporary gatehouse of St Andrews cathedral-priory.

Lindores Abbey, Fife

Founded by David Earl of Huntingdon, 1191. Said to have been colonised from Kelso. Although never the equal of the above-mentioned Tironensian houses it was of considerable importance, especially in the thirteenth century. It is now sadly ruined, and is known to have been used as a common quarry.[1] It had a short 'Cistercian' east end, transepts each with three eastern chapels, a nave which was aisled on the north side only[2] and a comparatively small cloister court which caused the south transept to encroach abnormally into the east range. A vaulted slype or passage through this range still remains, otherwise the buildings are reduced to their lower courses. Such fragments of detailing as are visible, in the slype and other parts, are of high quality craftsmanship in pure lancet gothic of the early thirteenth century. Parts of the precinct wall remain, including an entrance gateway.

This ruin is not in the Ministry's care.

CISTERCIAN HOUSES

Melrose Abbey, Roxburghshire

Founded by David I in 1136. The first Cistercian foundation in Scotland, and one of the largest in Britain. Colonised from Rievaulx abbey, Yorkshire. It suffered repeatedly in hostile border action: in 1322 Edward II caused great desolation, in 1385 Richard II burned and utterly destroyed it, in Hertford's invasion of 1545 it was sacked once more. From this it never fully recovered. It was revived as a Protestant church in 1618. The high barrel-vault over the west end of the choir dates from this time. The convent had two cloisters, one for the choir monks, the other for lay brothers. A main road passes over the western half of the lay brothers' cloister.

Nothing of the first church remains save the lower courses of its west wall, and of the contemporary cloistral buildings there are only low walls and foundations. They are nevertheless uncommonly instructive since almost the whole layout of the monastery is revealed. Clearly it was extensive

[1] See above, p. 57, for stone-robbing.
[2] A later modification? cf. Balmerino and Deer, pp. 78, 76.

even in its early days. But the upstanding remains which are admired today date from the late fourteenth to the sixteenth centuries.

The later church is extensive, and complete in many of its parts, with much vaulting intact and mouldings and carved details undamaged and unweathered. It dates from the reconstruction after Richard's invasion and continues until the sixteenth century. This post-1685 reconstruction is noticeably un-Scottish. French influences are inferred in the south transept, north of England influences more certainly in the east end (which could have been designed and hewn in the York masons' yard) while the two surviving crossing piers are closely paralleled in the contemporary work of the choir of Carlisle cathedral.

The arrangement of buildings around the cloisters repeats the normal layout but the cloisters are on the north side of the church. This is unconventional. They were placed on the north to ensure the essential flow of water for the reredorters or latrine chambers. The Tweed was dammed over a quarter mile west of the monastery. Through a lade the water drove the abbey mill, and was thence diverted along the great drain to flush the reredorter pits of the lay brothers' and the choir monks' ranges. The drain is five hundred feet long, four feet wide and five feet deep. It is an outstandingly good example. St Andrews cathedral-priory provides another.

High up in the north transept gable the rake of the dorter roof can be seen, and beneath it the night stair doorway. The chapter-house projected boldly to the east. It was in three aisles with two rows of piers for a ribbed vault. A few of the chapter-house floor tiles remain *in situ*. North of the chapter-house was the inner parlour, then the warming-house, and, in the corner, the day stair to the dorter. The north range consisted of the frater with the warming-house on one side, the kitchen on the other. The original twelfth-century frater lay parallel with the cloister alley, but the thirteenth-century frater was at right angles to it, extending far to the north, a noble room with central piers. Outside the frater was the *lavatorium*, or laver, projecting from the north cloister alley into the cloister court. This supplied running water for the washing of hands before meals, as monastic regulations required, by taps or fountain from a cistern or by a piped supply from other sources.[1] The basin was frequently a stone trough in the frater wall of the cloister walk, but in such a case as this it stood in a small detached or projecting building of no small architectural merit.

The lane or alley, characteristic of Cistercian planning where lay brothers were numerous, ran along the west side of the great cloister to divide it from the lay brothers' cloister and domestic ranges. Tanning pits are an interesting indication of a workaday activity. They occur also at the parent house of Rievaulx. In the north-east corner of the site, alongside the mill lade are the foundations of an abbot's hall of about 1246.

The original church had the characteristic short Cistercian choir. The existing (later) church followed the old plan but enlarged the transepts and presbytery and added a second south aisle to the nave. The great east window with the prickly and angular perpendicular tracery of the York school contrasts with the equally ambitious curvilinear window of French style in the south transept gable (Pls. 11 and 12). This was the work of John Morow (Moreau) whose posthumous credentials are engraved on a weathered stone plaque in the south transept which he designed and built. This memorial is unique. It testifies to the importance of the mediaeval master mason and the high regard in which he held himself, and which others had for him. (cf. a miniature tombstone effigy of a master mason with his tools in the museum of St Andrews cathedral.) A replica (restored) of the Morow plaque is in the abbey museum.

[1] Lead piping of the domestic water supply has been recovered, and is exhibited in the site museum. These systems were effective and often ingenious. Glenluce abbey still has its earthenware piping *in situ*. (See below, p. 76).

The twelfth-century cloister buildings long continued in use but the church which they served was demolished save for its west end, which remains some four feet high. Evidently the later church rose about its predecessor. The site was obviously not cleared when the new church was erected after the destruction of its predecessor. The remaining parts continued in use so that there would be no interruption in the performance of the Divine Office. (Holyrood was similarly rebuilt). Had the old west end been superseded it would of course have been utterly demolished, as otherwise it would have been an encumbrance in the interior of the later and longer church.

The foundations of the intended but never completed west end have been exposed and are dated by a coin, a denier of Charles VIII of France (1483-95). The original west wall is characteristically romanesque with squarish ashlars and flat pilaster buttresses. It has the simplest doorway in the middle, a narrow aperture with only chamfered edges as mouldings. It has no ornament, no decoration, no flanking columns. In its directness and stark simplicity this remarkable survival is a striking demonstration of the influence of early Cistercian ideals upon their architecture. It affords a telling contrast to the exuberance of the mouldings and sculptural enrichment of the church which later grew up round it. It is passed by without receiving more than a cursory glance, yet it is one of the most eloquent fragments of mediaeval architecture in Scotland.

Before the west wall an open arcaded porch or narthex was covered by a lean-to roof falling outwards from beneath the west windows. This was a traditional Cistercian feature, and a most unbecoming one at that, yet in its way indicative of the practical Cistercian outlook and its puritanical disregard for appearances. Evidence of these western entrance porches is also to be seen at Dundrennan and Sweetheart.

The Melrose sculptures are notable. Nowhere else in Scotland, save at the fifteenth-century collegiate church at Roslin, is there such profusion. Canopied niches and incidental sculpture of saintly and comical figures, grotesques, musicians, etc., are in great abundance (Pls. 14 and 15). Not only that, but as the church was rib-vaulted throughout (itself a notable achievement equalled only at Holyrood) carved vault bosses are numerous, and the capitals of piers and corbels are boldly moulded and sculptured with foliage. The great south buttress opposite the end of the ritual choir contains in its niche an effigy of the Virgin and Child to indicate and symbolise on the outside the beginning of the choir within.[1] A notable minor feature is the recurrent 'nodding-ogee', a sophisticated form of arch with an S-curve, whose apex overhangs to produce a rippling effect when repeated and seen sidelong—the arch is pulled out from the flat wall as it were, and achieves a three-dimensional effect (Pl. 15).

A second aisle was added to the south side of the nave, the north being impossible to modify because of the cloister, and along the south side there is a fine series of flying buttresses conducting the thrust of the high vault to the ground in two spans, one over each aisle. These are the only genuine mediaeval flying buttresses in Scotland.[2] The partial collapse of much of the vaulting affords opportunity of studying the mechanics of the structure.

The south aisle chapels are separated one from the other by solid stone walls rising from floor to vault, and each was separated from the aisle by a high timber screen. The lay brothers' choir was separated from the ritual choir by a massive stone pulpitum screen with a centre door flanked by two altars. The piers of the choir were joined by stone walls against which the choir stalls were placed. The screen walls

[1] After 1134 all Cistercian churches were dedicated to the Blessed Virgin Mary.

[2] Ornate flying buttresses occur at Roslin but they are illogical and demonstrate no awareness of the structural principles involved. For they push against a continuous barrel-vault and do not collect and resolve the convergent thrusts from various vault ribs. Flying buttresses were added to the walls of Holyrood and Dunfermline but they were emergency measures, not integral parts of a true vaulting system.

at Melrose provide unusually good evidence of the compartmentation of mediaeval churches.

For long before the Reformation the secularisation o monasteries had led to the king granting benefices *in commendam*. Such were originally temporary appointments of some person, frequently a layman, during a vacancy. The practice was much abused. Monastic funds were misappropriated by many a 'commendator' who regarded his appointment as a perquisite (which indeed it frequently was) and a fruitful source of personal income. The Commendator's House at Melrose has been restored for use as a museum for the many relics recovered during the clearance of the site, and from nearby houses and gardens. For comparison it exhibits items from other Cistercian houses in Scotland and Yorkshire. In an agreeable setting the museum displays a first-rate collection of mediaeval exhibits from all periods in the abbey's history—architectural fragments, stone sculpture, coins, pottery, tiles, etc.

The daughter houses of Melrose were Balmerino, Coupar Angus, Holmcultram, Kinloss and Newbattle.

Dundrennan Abbey, Kirkcudbrightshire
Founded by David I in 1142. Colonised from Rievaulx abbey, Yorkshire. The west wall of the church remains, with the great west doorway and corbels of the narthex roof. The nave is reduced to its lowest courses and the east gable of the church has entirely gone. The transept interiors, however, are well preserved and instructive examples of typical Cistercian gothic of the mid-twelfth century which combines structural pointed arcades with round arched windows (Pl. 17). This combination has been interpreted as an internal re-modelling within earlier outside walls which were retained. But there is no evidence in the masonry to support such a forced explanation of the co-existence of the pointed and round arches, and the explanation overlooks their co-existence in Cistercian churches in Yorkshire and France; at contemporary Kirkstall, and at Roche which was

completed before 1170, for example. Both employed the ribbed vault as Dundrennan does over the presbytery and the transept chapels, where the most important altars were. The exploitation at Dundrennan, at this date, of the pointed arch and ribbed vault signalises a notable advance in Scottish monastic architecture. Borrowed from contemporary French work in the districts where the Cistercians had strong affiliations this treatment of the structure contributed to the architectural prestige of the order whose influence was great, particularly in the north, and was not confined to houses of the order.

Towards the end of the thirteenth century, a new chapter-house was erected, much of which exists to illustrate the further departure from simplicity. Its west wall, in the cloister walk, is practically complete, with an exceedingly rich doorway flanked by the usual twin-light arched openings on either side of it. The chamber was in three aisles, with two rows of piers to carry a ribbed vault now unfortunately away. In the floor of the chapter-house lie several fine sculptured tombstones. This chapter-house is a remarkably successful exercise in decorated gothic. It far exceeds the simplicity and restraint of the earlier work, even to the use of surface enrichment, but the old refinement has not been forgotten, and the decorative effects are elegant and well placed. Compare it with the stark side walls of the unaisled presbytery, in which the Divine Office continued to be performed in the original architectural simplicity of more than a hundred years before.

The abbey was plundered as a quarry until 1842, when it was taken over and repaired by the Commissioners of Woods and Forests. It is now in the care of the Ministry.

It lies in a small secluded valley, near a stream, among trees, not far from the sea. It is remote but easy enough to reach by good roads which wind and undulate from Kirkcudbright, Castle Douglas and Dalbeattie. Its appearance is sudden and unexpected. No other abbey so eloquently expresses the ideals of the Cistercian brotherhood.

Glenluce Abbey, Wigtownshire
Founded 1191-2 by Roland, Lord of Galloway. Colonised
from Dundrennan. Of the nave little remains above foundation level save the south wall and the lower parts of the
west front. The south transept and fragmentary remains of
the choir stand high, with simple detail. The particular
attraction of Glenluce is its fine late fifteenth-century chapter
house, which is complete, a square apartment below ground
level covered by a ribbed vault rising from a central pier.
It was floored with glazed tiles many of which have been re-
set, and it is lit by two wide arched windows with tracery
similar to that in the chapter-house of Crossraguel.

The water supply system is a unique survival. Earthenware pipes, jointed and with inspection chambers lie in
their original positions where they are exposed to view. The
site has also yielded quantities of mediaeval pottery of late
thirteenth-century date which include high quality im-
ported French ware introduced by the wine trade in a
mediaeval continuation of the early prehistoric route up the
Irish Sea from the Atlantic coasts of France.

Culross Abbey, Fife
Founded by Malcolm Earl of Fife before 1217. Colonised
from Kinloss. The nave is demolished and a parish church
has been erected over the monastic choir. The foundations
and piers of the undercrofts of the east range and of the
frater remain. There is much excellent detail to be observed
but the conception of a great monastery is somewhat difficult
to appreciate because of the dramatic changes in ground
levels and the fragmentary nature of the surviving parts.

Deer Abbey, Aberdeenshire
Founded by William Cumyn, Earl of Buchan, 1219.
Colonised from Kinloss. The church was totally demolished
in the nineteenth century. The plan is indicated by foundations. The church had apparently only one aisle, on its
north side. The position of the west door and the alignment

of the choir suggest that although of late date in Cistercian history it might originally have been of the primitive Cistercian plan without aisles.[1] If that were so, and with cloisters lying against its south side, enlargement would be possible only on the north. The plan was also out of date in placing the frater parallel with the south cloister alley. The foundations of the cloistral buildings indicate that the community could never have been large. The infirmary and the abbot's house have been identified to the south-east of the church. The south range of the cloister stands high and has been considerably altered. There was a Celtic monastery of the Columban mission at Deer. It is renowned for the *Book of Deer*, one of the most precious literary relics of the Celtic church. Although in the neighbourhood, the site of the Celtic settlement is not likely to have been that of the mediaeval house, as the Cistercians sought virgin sites.[2]

Sweetheart Abbey, Kirkcudbrightshire

Founded by Devorgilla, wife of John Balliol of Barnard Castle in 1273. The last Cistercian foundation in Scotland. Colonised from Dundrennan. A very substantial ruin. The nave arcades are complete to the top of the clerestory and the south aisle wall stands high. On its cloister side may be seen the projecting corbels which supported the roof of the north cloister. The great west front and the east gable of the choir are also complete (Pl. 21).

The transepts stand high all round and still carry a crossing tower. Although by reputation one of the most beautiful monastic ruins one must confess nevertheless that the effect is somewhat fortuitous and the architecture not all that it might be. Much of the charm of the building is due to the colourful contrast of the red sandstone, the green expanses of grass, and the spacious blue of the sky—and also to the fortunate completeness of the church. The detailing of the window tracery is poor. The depressed arches of the nave arcade and, particularly, of the great eastern window,

[1] See below, pp. 90-1.   [2] See above, p. 54.

are especially unhappy. However, there is some good work to be seen and all is interesting even if only to compare with nearby Dundrennan. The south transept window is of interest as an example of the way the mediaeval mason contrived to adjust his fenestration to the encroachment of the east range against the transept gable. The cloistral ranges are greatly ruined and not of much account. An isolated doorway on the line of the presumed inner wall of the west range faces west, which suggests that the wall in which it stood was in fact a free-standing outer wall, and that there was in fact no western range. A similar wall existed in place of a west range at Dryburgh. Outside the west gable, beneath the great window and over the doorway, are the corbels of the lean-to roof which covered the narthex, that characteristic feature of Cistercian churches.

The abbey was enclosed by an extensive precinct wall of exceedingly large unhewn boulders. Considerable stretches of this remarkable cyclopean masonry survive in good height and, like the abbey, are in the care of the Ministry.

The following are Cistercian houses in Scotland of which some remains might be seen, but which are not in the care of the Ministry of Public Building and Works.

Balmerino Abbey, Fife
Founded by the widow of William the Lion and her son, Alexander II, *c* 1227. Colonised from Melrose. Little remains of church or cloisters save a vaulted chapter-house and adjoining parts of the east range. The cloisters were placed on the north of the church which had a south aisle only. This suggests that the church was originally aisleless.[1]

Coupar Angus Abbey, Angus
Founded by Malcolm IV *c* 1164 from Melrose. Of this house only a fragment of a gatehouse survives. In the parish

[1] cf. Lindores, p. 68, and Deer, p. 76.

church which was erected on the site of the monastic church are the remains of nave piers.

Newbattle Abbey, Midlothian

Founded by David I in association with his son, Earl Henry, in 1140. Colonised from Melrose. Foundations of a large church and extensive cloistral buildings have been uncovered from time to time, but the only visible part of the monastery is the ground floor of its east range, now incorporated in Newbattle Abbey College. This work is extremely fine with notable ribbed vaults. The site of the monastic church has yielded fine sets of decorative glazed tiles to be compared with those from the parent house of Melrose and the Yorkshire house of Byland.

Kinloss Abbey, Moray

Founded by David I in 1150, from Melrose. Much ruined. The extent of the cloister has been discovered, but the only upstanding masonry of note is part of the south transept and an adjacent vaulted chamber, and an arched entrance to the cloister on its south side, besides which is a rare surviving example of a laver within an arched recess. Remains of a detached abbot's house of a late period overlie a well preserved extent of the reredorter drain.

Saddell Abbey, Argyll

Founded by Reginald, son of Somerled, Lord of the Isles, *c* 1207. Mother-house unknown. This monastery is greatly ruined.

AUGUSTINIAN HOUSES

Inchcolm Abbey, Fife

On an island in the Forth, founded by Alexander I *c* 1123. The island has an early Christian history and the mediaeval church may well have been erected over a Celtic settlement. The substantial ruins of the church date from the twelfth century and are much involved by frequent additions and alterations up to the fifteenth century. The structure of the church is thereby somewhat difficult to understand, but it contains some interesting features, notably a pulpitum screen and a portion of a painted plaster fresco depicting the burial of a canon. The cloister is small but complete, all three domestic ranges being roofed. A peculiarity of the cloisters is that they do not lie beneath a lean-to roof outside the surrounding buildings but are included in the buildings as basements opening to the cloister court. The cloister arcade is in fact a series of windows with window seats in the basements of the three surrounding ranges. The chapter-house is octagonal, unique in monastic work and paralleled in Scotland only at Elgin cathedral. It follows an English fashion of the second half of the thirteenth century.

Holyrood Abbey, Edinburgh

Founded by David 1 in 1128. A great mediaeval abbey absorbed into the seventeenth-century palace of Holyrood-house. The east end and transepts are reduced to rubble foundations and the cloistral buildings are entirely de-molished, but the greater part of the thirteenth-century nave exists. It was an elegant and ambitious structure, impressive still, despite the disconcerting and misleading gothic-survival window which filled the west crossing-arch in 1633, to close and separate the nave from the ruined transepts and choir beyond. The nave (Pl. 20) was stone-vaulted through-out, and that in itself was a notable achievement. Only one other monastic church, Melrose of the early fifteenth century, aspired to such constructional bravura. But am-bitious though they were, the masons of the thirteenth century did not disdain the pedestrian romanesque, and into no less than five bays of the north aisle wall they incorporated sequences of fine inter-laced wall-arcading inherited from the earlier church.

Holyrood abbey was in process of growth and alteration for some one hundred and fifty years, new parts being erected round the existing parts which continued in use so that essential services would not be interrupted.[1] Of the original church nothing remains but a rebuilt east processional doorway and foundations beneath the site of the thirteenth-century aisled choir. The later north wall-arcade referred to above represents a twelfth-century enlargement of the original unaisled church whose nave foundations lie wholly within the existing nave. A comprehensive rebuilding of the entire church began *c* 1220 and continued steadily until the fourteenth century.

The early thirteenth-century rebuilding was very good indeed, particularly the west front, an imposing façade with a deeply recessed doorway which was flanked by boldly projecting towers. The south tower was demolished to make way for the palace but the north tower is complete to the wallhead. Its 'show-façades', the west and south sides, bear two tiers of decorative wall arches. Between the arches of the lower sequence is a series of fine circular portrait medallions in high relief. This west front, although mutilated and lacking the essential south tower, is to be numbered among the most imaginative and successful exercises in early thirteenth-century composition in Britain (Pl. 19).

Over the doorway were two large windows, ingeniously contrived with double tracery, the dominating feature of the gable end between the towers. They contained a tribune gallery or galilee porch, an arresting feature derived from liturgical ceremony which occurred in different forms at Arbroath and St Andrews. When Charles I in 1633 decided that his coronation should take place in the abbey church the ruined building was put to rights and the west front was finished off on baroque lines for which there is evidence in modifications which are particularly noticeable at the window heads.

Jedburgh Abbey, Roxburghshire
Founded by David I *c* 1138. Colonised probably from Beauvais. On a sloping site the buildings descended in

[1] As at Melrose: see above, p. 72.

terraces to the River Jed. Unquestionably the most interesting part of Jedburgh is the presbytery of imaginative
and unorthodox design, a variation of the normal and logical
expression of the three principal stages of the internal elevations, main arcade, triforium passage, and clerestory which
are here dramatised by the use of giant cylindrical piers
rising from the ground to carry the triforium arch (Pl. 25).
The triforium floor is in effect slung across the space between
the piers and the main arches spring from corbels half-way
up the piers. It is rarely that the mediaeval mason took
liberties like this with his structure.

The short transepts had apsidal ends. The cloistral
buildings are ruined but extensive and in places they stand
quite high. The west front is one of the finest transitional or
late twelfth-century elevations in Scotland (Pl. 24). The
entrance doorway is recessed in a projecting porch and its
arched orders are lavishly decorated with characteristic
romanesque detail, chevrons, bird's beak, billet mouldings,
etc. The porch is surmounted by three pedimented gables
with three niches for statues. Above this in the main west
wall is a lofty round arched window flanked by a wall-
arcade of small pointed arches upon exceedingly long slender
shafts engaged to the wall.

The nave elevations are complete, and drawn with a more
assured grasp of the new gothic forms. Yet the conception of
the triforium, with its large tribune opening spanning the bay
is reminiscent of the romanesque, even if the round arch is
subdivided by two smaller lancets upon slender clustered
shafts. The rhythm of the clerestory arcade is very different,
much more rapid, with an uninterrupted horizontal run of
lancets in a repeating pattern of solid and void.

Cambuskenneth Abbey, Stirlingshire

Founded by David 1 *c* 1140. Colonised from Arrouaise. The
only part of the church which survives to any height is the
western doorway, the walls are reduced to their lower
courses. The church was cruciform, with an aisle on the

north side only. The chapter-house was vaulted from a central pier, the frater was parallel with the south cloister alley. The architecture of the site is represented by a complete and notable campanile or bell tower, a detached structure for which there are no parallels in Scotland. It rises sixty-seven feet over a vaulted basement. There are good lancet windows and an ornamental arcade of lancets round the outside. It is an excellent example of thirteenth-century architecture (Pl. 28).

James III and his queen were buried beside the high altar in 1485, and what is believed to be a part of the royal tomb was uncovered during excavations in 1864. This, a large slab of blue stone, is the only fragment of a mediaeval royal tomb in Scotland. In 1865 the royal remains were re-interred beneath a memorial on the site of the high altar at the command and expense of Her Majesty Queen Victoria (who also caused the desecrated royal remains in Holyrood abbey to be re-interred).

St Andrew's Cathedral-Priory, Fife

Founded by Robert, Bishop of St Andrews, 1144. Colonised from Scone. One of the two Scottish cathedrals served by regular clergy, the other being the Premonstratensian Whithorn. The church was one of the largest in Britain. The present building was begun about 1160. The choir was completed by 1238 in which year Bishop Malvoisin was buried in it. The original west end was demolished in a great storm and the present work was erected two bays to the east of it *c* 1280 thus shortening the nave. The north wall of the nave has been reduced to its lowest courses but the south is complete to the wallhead. The east gable (Pl. 26) is the only twelfth-century east gable to survive in height, but its original fenestration has been disturbed by the insertion of the large fifteenth-century traceried window. The lower parts of the aisled chancel were enriched by wall arcading similar to that on the west wall of the south transept. There were many distinguished personages interred in the choir and chancel.

Recumbent effigies upon decorated tombs, beneath arched recesses, are commonplace in mediaeval churches. Their survival hides the underlying structure. In the chancel of St Andrews the opposite is the case. The upper-works have gone and the empty stone sepulchres which contained the coffins are exposed.

The cloister is large and lacks its west range. The east range is well preserved. The south range consists only of the undercroft of the frater. A once arcaded slype or passage skirts the south transept gable. Next to the slype is the chapter-house, originally square with four piers, later extended eastwards, when it became vestibule to its successor. The warming-house was restored in the late nineteenth century. It has recently been re-fashioned as a site museum for the collection of early Christian stones, mediaeval relics and a superb sarcophagus of late ninth or early tenth-century date which has no parallel in Britain or indeed in Western Europe, an outstanding example of Dark Age art. It undoubtedly contained relics of no ordinary importance, of King Constantine perhaps, the only early Scottish king known not to have been interred on Iona, or even of St Regulus, or St Andrew himself. It has been restored and occupies a place of honour in the museum. It suggests an explanation of the strange church known as St Rule's, or St Regulus', which stands a few yards from the east end of the mediaeval church.

St Regulus' church (Pl. 27) has hitherto been considered the original St Andrews cathedral, *ie* the predecessor of the ruined cathedral. A cathedral-priory church would surely have been somewhat different, however, and more suited to the requirements of the monastic life and the round of divine service than this is. The simple arrangement of tower, short choir, and apse would be most inconvenient for monastic cathedral services. Another explanation might be advanced: it is not unlikely that St Regulus' church was in fact a reliquary church, especially built for the sarcophagus and the holy relics.

Monastic precinct or mantle walls are rare survivals today, although once frequent as a protection and as a symbol of enclosure, a separation of the monastery from the outside world just as the Celtic cashel wall was. They exist in extent elsewhere only at Pluscarden and Sweetheart. The St Andrews example is incomparably the finest. It was rebuilt by Prior Hepburn in the first quarter of the sixteenth century and equipped with towers and gun-ports upon earlier foundations of which evidence can be seen. It follows an extensive circuit, entirely surrounding the monastery, two cemeteries, a gas works, and St Leonard's School for girls and its playing fields. It finished at the great gatehouse of the early fourteenth century. Apart from that at Arbroath abbey this is the only surviving gatehouse in Scotland.

In the museum and in the undercroft of the frater there are as good restorations of mediaeval vaulted cellarage as can be found.

Restenneth Priory, Angus

Founded by Malcolm IV about 1153. Historical probability of a preceding foundation on this site is supported by an unusual square tower of archaic form which is the ruin's most conspicuous feature. The tower stands at the west end of a thirteenth-century unaisled choir into which it is wholly incorporated, in much the same way as an early romanesque square tower was included in the thirteenth-century cathedral of Dunblane. Of the nave of the mediaeval church which was built around the tower only foundations remain, but the cloisters on the south are indicated by high walls on their west and south sides and some foundations of the east range. The tower exhibits unusual pre-romanesque features and seems to have been a western tower of a narrow church of Saxon type. The south wall of the thirteenth-century choir probably stands upon the south wall of the nave of the earlier church. The alignment of the arched passage through the tower—a sort of chancel arch in the later church—suggests that the north wall of the early church was demolished, as tending to make its successor too narrow. The primitive detailing of the tower's doorway is paralleled in Scotland only at the round tower of Abernethy, an Irish Celtic form with romanesque modifications datable to about 1050.

Inchmahome Priory, Perthshire

Founded by Walter, Earl of Montieth, 1238. A small house beautifully situated on an island in the Lake of Monteith. The church is fragmentary but parts stand high including the east gable. The cloistral buildings are also fragmentary and the chapter-house, a simple oblong, is complete and contains an interesting effigy of a knight and his lady side by side.

The choir is unaisled, the nave has a north aisle, probably an extension. The choir was unusually well lit with five tall lancets in its east gable and double light windows on either side. The detailing is all of thirteenth century date with much resemblance to that on the nearby cathedral of Dunblane. The western door is particularly fine, being a large opening deeply recessed beneath multiple mouldings and flanked by side shafts. It is supported on either side by twin lancets with trefoil and quatrefoil openings in the spandrels. There are also unusually fine sedilia in the south wall of the choir.

In 1543 Mary Queen of Scots as a child found refuge here along with her mother after the battle of Pinkie and resided in the convent for some months before departing for France.

PREMONSTRATENSIAN HOUSES

Dryburgh Abbey, Berwickshire

Founded by Hugh de Morville in 1150. Colonised from Alnwick. Little of the nave survives above the foundation courses, save for its south wall, but the gable of the south transept is complete to its apex, and the celebrated fragment of the east end which enshrines the tombs of Field-Marshal Earl Haig and Sir Walter Scott, the vaulted north transeptal chapels and the north choir aisle (Pl. 29), is an excellent example of restrained but imaginative design characteristic of the best thirteenth-century work.

The Scottish partiality for horizontal emphasis in the interior elevations is here rejected. The bays are strongly marked by wall-shafts which run up from the capitals of the main arcade. The triforium is compressed, and this important *motif* of the internal elevation (its omission at Melrose is a serious deficiency in that design) is expressed not by arcading but by a single quatrefoil opening in each bay, a sort of architectural punctuation mark between the main and the clerestory arcades. By this unconventional treatment extravagance of height is avoided while the main arcade receives full value and the clerestory more than its usual value.

The nave was extended in the fifteenth century at which time the round arch was being revived by Scottish masons, particularly for use in doorways. Simultaneously, there was a fashionable quickening of detail by a flattening or reduction in the projection of capitals and bases, or by their elimination altogether. The new west doorway at Dryburgh might not be entirely pleasing to eyes which appreciate the pure and logical forms of the north transeptal chapels described above, and the notes of sculptural interest with which it is embellished might not appear to ring so truly as they do in the earlier work, but it is a valuable and interesting fragment of the fifteenth century for all that. The arch mouldings sweep without interruption down to the base: the accustomed side shafts have become a downward extension of the all-important arch, and the intervening capitals are abolished altogether in an inevitable architectural evolution—yet the the bases remain, albeit without their former projection which suggested a proper stability.

The cloistral remains are extensive, the east range being

the finest in Scotland (Pls. 31 and 32). The chapter-house is a good example of its kind, a simple barrel-vaulted unaisled chamber with benching and a wall arcade of intersecting arches. It bears much evidence of painted wall surfaces, plastered white with imitation jointing in red, and of other decorative devices such as chevrons, foliage, etc.

From the late twelfth-century east processional doorway in the angle of the nave and the south transept the full sequence of apartments is revealed without interruption along its entire length. From the church southwards we have a deep book-cupboard grooved for shelves, sacristy and library, inner parlour, chapter-house, and day stair to the dorter on the first floor. The extension of this range beyond the south range is considerable: the ground falls away steeply to the south, and at the south end of the east cloister walk a flight of steps descends to its undercrofts. An aisled warming-house, a barrel-vaulted passage to the infirmary and cemetery beyond these dwellings to the east, and an aisled hall bring the range to a wide water channel which served the reredorter. Of this and the dorter little remains. The night stair doorway high in the south transept gable opened from the dorter into the south transept, and to the night stair which was set against the transept's west wall. The west gable and undercrofts of the frater survive on the south side. There was no west range, but instead an enclosing wall.

In its unspoiled rural setting among trees this is one of our most attractive monuments, dramatically set off by the fall of ground.

Whithorn Cathedral-Priory, Wigtownshire

The importance of the historic early Christian monastery is described elsewhere in this volume.[1] The monastery probably declined during the period of Viking domination which ended *c*1100 in these parts. Soon after this Fergus

[1] See above, p. 12 and pp. 17-19.

Lord of Galloway followed the current of religious revival and the building of great churches by re-establishing the lapsed bishopric. Gilla-Aldan the first bishop of the new succession was consecrated *c* 1128. The romanesque cathedral, of which some notable but fragmentary parts survive, is of his time. This church was an equal-armed cruciform, unlike the long aisled churches of the new monastic orders but very like contemporary churches which were similarly being erected upon Celtic monastic sites in Wales.

Gilla-Aldan's successor, Bishop Christian, who was consecrated in 1154, was a supporter of the Premonstratensian order of regular canons. These he introduced to serve his cathedral church just as the Augustinians were introduced to serve the cathedral priory of St Andrews about the same time. Whithorn was thus, like St Andrews, a monastery whose church served as the cathedral church of the diocese. For the Premonstratensians a new church was erected in the early thirteenth century. It was erected upon the site of the old church, doubled the length of its nave, and incorporated parts of its predecessor in its fabric. The fine romanesque doorway at the west end of the nave is a notable thirteenth-century re-use of a twelfth-century doorway. The nave bears witness to late alterations.

The east end of the Premonstratensian church is exceedingly long and advances over sloping ground to overlie the ruins of St Ninian's historic church whose foundations are to be seen emerging from beneath its east gable wall. Whithorn was a renowned place of pilgrimage throughout the Middle Ages. It is very probable that on the east side of the monastic high altar there was a shrine containing the relics of the saint. This would lie over the original church where his body and those of many saints were laid to rest almost eight hundred years before. Such reliquary chambers were suitable for the pilgrim traffic and in this position symbolised the elevation of the soul of the departed saint.

SA G

Recent excavations at Whithorn in the vicinity of the high altar, undertaken as part of needful consolidation, have yielded the graves of three distinguished prelates who were interred in state. They had been buried in rich vestments, with buckled belts and finger rings, and lay with croziers and chalices. This is perhaps the most important grave group of the mediaeval period which has been systematically examined in Scotland.

Adjacent to the monument is a site museum containing early Christian and mediaeval relics.

VALLISCAULIAN HOUSES

Ardchattan Priory, Argyll

Founded by Sir Duncan Macdougall of Lorn in 1230. Of the domestic buildings little can be said, as they have been demolished or incorporated in a modern mansion. The fragmentary east end of the church and parts of its transepts have survived and show good quality work, the more note-worthy on account of its remoteness. With the nearby late twelfth-century chapel at Dunstaffnage castle and the thir-teenth-century cathedral church on the island of Lismore, whose fragmentary remains are incorporated in the modern parish church, Ardchattan represents the European tra-dition in mediaeval architecture in the mainland of the western highlands.

Beauly Priory, Inverness-shire

Founded by John Bisset and ? Alexander II, 1230. The walls of the church are intact but roofless. There is good minor detail and interesting fenestration. A small compact cloister on the south is now entirely gone. The original form was a long unaisled nave with short unaisled transepts and a choir which was a continuation of the nave. It recalls the most primitive Cistercian plan of Waverley, the first house of that order in Britain (1128-9). It also recalls the unaisled nave

and choir of Deer abbey[1] another late house of early plan
from which Beauly might have been derived.

Pluscarden Priory, Moray

Founded by Alexander II in 1230. United to the Benedictine
Urquhart in 1453/4 because its strength had fallen to six
monks, Urquhart's to two. It then became a Benedictine
house. The nave was apparently never raised upon its
foundations. Choir and transepts are largely intact, and
extensive cloistral remains survive. The scale, the design of
the building, and the excellence of its detailing establish the
east end and transepts of Pluscarden among the finest
achievements of a notable period. After desertion and decay
the monastery has in recent years been re-occupied by a
small community of Benedictines. The manner in which
they have returned after an absence of more than three
hundred and fifty years, and the events which have led up to
their return, are worth relating here, for, with due regard
to modern influences, the circumstances must be typical of
many a mediaeval colonisation.

In the early years of the present century two Carthusian
monks came from France to inspect the ruined and deserted
priory with a view to acquiring it as a dependent house. The
cost of restoration being prohibitive the Carthusian proposal
was inevitably abandoned. In 1920 Lord Calum Crichton-
Stuart offered it to the Benedictines of Caldey Island in
South Wales, but at that time Caldey could ill afford the
loss of monks necessary for such a pioneer adventure. Years
later further appeals were made to Caldey and to other
communities, and were perforce declined because of the
great cost of restoration and the availability of other
suitable buildings to meet the needs of expansion. As Lord
Calum made his third appeal to Prinknash abbey he had
decided that, should it fail, he would offer the ruins to the
then Office of Works (now the Ministry of Public Building
and Works) as an Ancient Monument. The occasion was

[1] See above, p. 76.

this time propitious. Prinknash accepted, and in 1948 an advance party of six monks journeyed from England to reoccupy their priory. The monks in Pluscarden today live and worship in makeshift fashion as best they can in the ruins of the monastery they have revived and are rebuilding, an undertaking quite in the mediaeval spirit.

Bibliography

Among the many published works to which the present
author is indebted in the preparation of this volume, par-
ticular acknowledgment is due to the following: 'Scottish
Rulers and the Religious Orders,' by G. W. S. Barrow,
Eng. Hist. Rev., vol. III (1953), 77-100; *Mediaeval Religious
Houses: Scotland*, by D. E. Easson, Longmans, 1957; *Early
Christian Ireland*, by Maire and Liam de Paor, Thames &
Hudson, 1958; *The Origin of the Austin Canons and their
Introduction into England*, by J. C. Dickinson, Oxford Press,
1950; *The White Canons in England*, by H. M. Colvin, Oxford
Press, 1951; *Pleasure of Ruins*, by Rose Macaulay, Weidenfeld
& Nicolson, 1953; *English Monastic Life*, by F. A. Gasquet,
Methuen, 1905; *Mediaeval Panorama*, by G. G. Coulton,
Cambridge University Press, 1943; *Life of Ailred of Rievaulx*,
by Walter Daniel, ed. F. M. Powicke, Cambridge Uni-
versity Press, 1950; *The Monastic Order in England*, by M. D.
Knowles, Cambridge University Press, 1949; *The Beginnings
of English Society*, by Dorothy Whitelock, Penguin Books,
1954; *Abbeys*, by M. R. James, Great Western Railway,
1925; *L'Architecture Cistercienne en France*, by M. Aubert,
Paris, 1947.

Acknowledgments

Permission has been given for quotation to be made from the following works: *Scottish Abbeys and Social Life*, by G. G. Coulton, Cambridge University Press, 1933; 'Eileach an Naoimh Reconsidered', by W. Douglas Simpson, *Scottish Gaelic Studies*, vol. VIII (1958), 117-129; *English Society in the Early Middle Ages*, by D. M. Stenton, Penguin Books, 1952; *Early Christian Irish Art*, by Francoise Henry, Dublin, 1954; *Feudal Britain*, by G. W. S. Barrow, Edward Arnold, 1956; *Bede: A History of the English Church and People*, by Leo Sherley-Price, Penguin Books, 1955.

Appendix

These are the Scottish monastic sites in the guardianship of the Secretary of State for Scotland and cared for and maintained on his behalf by the Ministry of Public Building and Works as Ancient Monuments, arranged in counties.

Aberdeenshire
  Deer (Cistercian)
Angus
  Arbroath (Tironensian)
  Restenneth (Augustinian)
Argyll
  Ardchattan (Valliscaulian)
Ayrshire
  Crossraguel (Cluniac)
Berwickshire
  Dryburgh (Premonstratensian)
Fife
  Culross (Cistercian)
  Dunfermline (Benedictine)
  Inchcolm (Augustinian)
  St Andrews (Augustinian)
Inverness-shire
  Beauly (Valliscaulian)
Kirkcudbrightshire
  Dundrennan (Cistercian)
  Sweetheart (Cistercian)
Midlothian
  Holyrood (Augustinian)
Perthshire
  Inchmahome (Augustinian)

Roxburghshire
  Jedburgh (Augustinian)
  Kelso (Tironensian)
  Melrose (Cistercian)
Stirlingshire
  Cambuskenneth (Augustinian of Arrouaise)
Wigtownshire
  Glenluce (Cistercian)
  Whithorn (Premonstratensian)

*   *   *

For most monuments official guide books and postcards
are available. The monuments are open to the public daily.
Details of admission and location are to be found in the
Illustrated Guide to the Ancient Monuments of Scotland, HMSO
(1970) price 10s (50p) hard cover; 6s (30p) paperback by
Professor Stuart Piggott (prehistoric periods) and the late
Dr W. Douglas Simpson (mediaeval and later periods). The
volume includes a section, arranged in counties, which gives
brief descriptions of all the two hundred and eighty Scottish monuments in the Ministry's care, with useful information about access and admission. It is illustrated and
has a distribution map. Complementary to this present
volume is *Abbeys: An Introduction to the Religious Houses of
England and Wales*, HMSO (1958) price 5s (25p) by
R. Gilyard-Beer, the Inspector of Ancient Monuments for
England.

PLATE 1 *Dunfermline, the west front*

PLATE 2 *Dunfermline, the nave*

PLATE 3 *Coldingham, the choir*

PLATE 4 *Paisley, the nave*

PLATE 5 *Crossraguel, view across the cloister court*

PLATE 6 *Kelso, the nave*

PLATE 7 *Kelso, the north transept*

PLATE 8 *Arbroath, the west front and gatehouse range*

PLATE 9 *Arbroath, the nave interior, looking to the west end*

PLATE 10 *Arbroath, the south transept*

PLATE II *Melrose, the east gable*

PLATE 12 *Melrose, the south side*

PLATE 13 *Melrose, conjectural restoration*

PLATE 14 *Melrose, pig playing bagpipes*

PLATE 15 *Melrose, niche and grotesques*

PLATE 16 *Dundrennan, conjectural restoration*

PLATE 17 *Dundrennan, view across the cloister court*

PLATE 18 *Dundrennan, the north transept chapels*

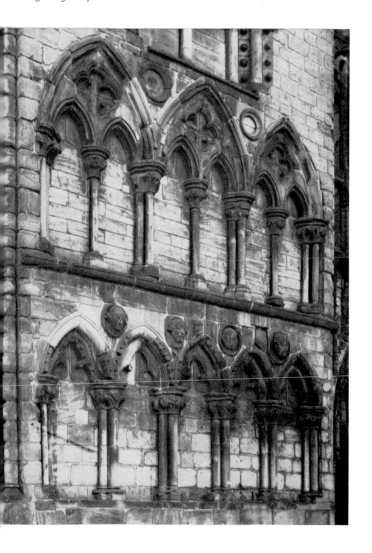

PLATE 21 *Sweetheart, from the north-west*

PLATE 22 *Jedburgh, conjectural restoration*

PLATE 23 *Jedburgh, the south side from the west cloister*

PLATE 24 *Jedburgh, the west front*

PLATE 25 *Jedburgh, the choir*

PLATE 26 *St. Andrews Cathedral-priory, the east gable*

PLATE 27 *St. Regulus' Church, St Andrews*

PLATE 28 *Cambuskenneth, the detached belfry*

PLATE 29 *Dryburgh, the north transept*

PLATE 30 *Dryburgh, conjectural restoration*

PLATE 31 *Dryburgh, the east range and south transept gable*

PLATE 32 *Dryburgh, detail of east range, the chapter-house entrance*

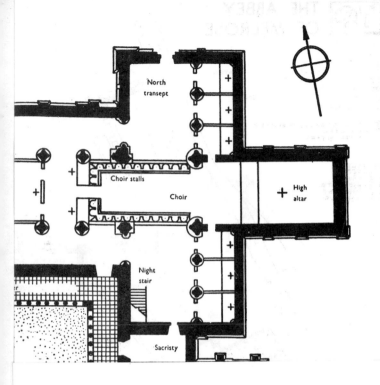

North
transept

Choir stalls

Choir

High
altar

Night
stair

Sacristy

SUBJECT TO
AS FURTHER
FOUNDATIONS
OVERED

CH
1
2
3
4
5